JUDGE & PUNISH

Photo: Courtroom, United States Courthouse, Davenport, Iowa. Source: Library of Congress, Prints & Photographs Division, photograph by Carol M. Highsmith [LC-DIG-pplot-13725-01364 (digital file from LC-HS503-489)].

GEOFFROY DE LAGASNERIE

JUDGE & PUNISH

THE PENAL STATE ON TRIAL

Translated by Lara Vergnaud

STANFORD UNIVERSITY PRESS • STANFORD, CALIFORNIA

Stanford University Press
Stanford, California

English translation © 2018 by the Board of Trustees of the Leland Stanford Junior University. All rights reserved.

Judge and Punish: The Penal State on Trial was originally published in French in 2016 under the title *Juger: L'État pénal face à la sociologie* © 2016, Librairie Arthème Fayard.

This work received support from the French Ministry of Foreign Affairs and the Cultural Services of the French Embassy in the United States through their publishing assistance program.

No part of this book may be reproduced or transmitted in any form or by any means, electronic or mechanical, including photocopying and recording, or in any information storage or retrieval system without the prior written permission of Stanford University Press.

Printed in the United States of America on acid-free, archival-quality paper

Library of Congress Cataloging-in-Publication Data

Names: Lagasnerie, Geoffroy de, author. | Vergnaud, Lara, translator.
Title: Judge and punish : the penal state on trial / Geoffroy de Lagasnerie ; [translated by] Lara Vergnaud.
Other titles: Juger. English
Description: Stanford, California : Stanford University Press, 2018. | Translation of: Juger : L'État pénal face à la sociologie. | Includes bibliographical references.
Identifiers: LCCN 2017049713 (print) | LCCN 2017052140 (ebook) | ISBN 9781503605794 (e-book) | ISBN 9781503601925 (cloth : alk. paper) | ISBN 9781503605787 (pbk. : alk. paper)
Subjects: LCSH: Sociological jurisprudence. | Law—Philosophy. | Criminal justice, Administration of—Philosophy.
Classification: LCC K371 (ebook) | LCC K371 .L3413 2018 (print) | DDC 340/.115—dc23
LC record available at https://lccn.loc.gov/2017049713

Cover design: Rob Ehle
Typeset by Bruce Lundquist in 11.25/16 Adobe Garamond Pro

For D., of course

CONTENTS

PART ONE: WHAT WE ARE

1 The State on Trial — 3
2 Subjects of the Law: A Repressive Theory of Power — 13
3 From Law to Critique — 19

PART TWO: THE STATE AND VIOLENCE

4 Civilization and Its Lies — 29
5 See the State for What It Is — 35
6 The Double Reality of Violence — 43

PART THREE: THE SYSTEM OF JUDGMENT

7 Beyond Responsibility — 67
8 The Politics of Perceptions — 80
9 An Individualizing Narrative — 99
10 React Differently — 118

PART FOUR: THE SYSTEM OF PUNISHMENT

11 Accuse and Punish — 135

12	The Logic of Punishment	146
13	What Is a Crime? The Fictional Frameworks of Penality	159
14	Penality, Sovereignty, and Democracy	172

PART FIVE: SEE THE WORLD

| 15 | Rethink Sociology | 193 |

JUDGE & PUNISH

PART ONE
WHAT WE ARE

THE STATE ON TRIAL

Here in this room, or really any other similar room, in any case a room laid out in the same way, filled with the same people playing the same roles and performing the same functions, I've seen individuals accused, and convicted, of robbery, assault, first- and second-degree murder, manslaughter, piracy, false imprisonment, and rape. Almost all of them were men. Almost all came from disenfranchised classes or lived in low-income and marginalized environments. The proportion of nonwhites (blacks, North Africans, Asians) and foreigners (Poles, Indians, Serbs, Somalis, etc.) immediately struck me as considerable.

Statistics have always confirmed the overrepresentation of dominated groups among the accused. Around 6 percent of the French population is composed of foreigners, compared to around 12 percent of the country's convicted criminals. Official statistics don't include information on the class origins of individuals being tried. There is little doubt, however—and this is confirmed by existing studies—that delinquents belong overwhelmingly to lower socioeconomic classes. For example, an estimated 95 percent of murders are committed by "persons belonging to the working classes, or even to the most underprivileged social strata."[1] That ratio also applies to the majority of countries in Europe and to the United States. Men represent approximately 90 percent of those convicted.

These observations conceal a reality that should guide any analysis of the criminal justice system and that dooms to error any undertaking that doesn't take it into account: there is a social mechanism behind confrontations with the justice system, that is, behind acts that expose people to the state's punitive apparatus. The existence of a social logic of illegal activity is not a hypothesis, an isolated perspective, or a debatable opinion. It is a fact. The truth. This thereby justifies, and even demands, an understanding of crimes and criminals based on social theory and, by extension, a social critique of justice and penality.

The first feeling that came over me when I began to observe court proceedings in France was, for the above reason, one of unease. As soon as you enter a courtroom, the reality that the acts being judged are determined by broader social contexts, which should allow them, at least in part, to be understood and explained, is completely suppressed and ignored—kept at a distance, in other words. Any sociological perception of individuals is refused. The slightest attempt to comprehend the cause of their actions is deemed irrelevant to the point that when certain mechanisms or variables— gender, race, class, age—are mentioned, notably by defense lawyers, their importance is dismissed. ("Come now, poor people aren't all thieves" is a typical phrase that judges and prosecutors like to say,

---

1. For a sociological study of this topic see Laurent Mucchielli, "Demographic and Social Characteristics of Murderers and Their Victims: A Survey on a Département of the Paris Region in the 1990s" (www.laurent-mucchielli.org/public/Article_Population_version_anglaise.pdf). The article is a translation of "Les caractéristiques démographiques et sociales des meurtriers et de leurs victimes: Une enquête sur un département de la région parisienne dans les années 1990," *Population* 59, no. 2 (2004): 203–32. See also Angèle Christin, *Comparutions immédiates* (Paris: La Découverte, 2008).

along with "Just because somebody drinks doesn't mean he'll become violent" or "You're insulting all poor people by saying that.")

WALLS

The legal system is built on a fundamental hypocrisy, the strength of which is obvious in a small courtroom, Room 2 in Paris's Palais de Justice,* which I visited on numerous occasions. A single, short wall separates the clerk's area of the court from the room in which proceedings take place. On one side of the wall is posted a list of upcoming trials on which the first and last names of the accused reveal, in this case, the overwhelming presence of ethnic minorities. Yet on the other side of the wall, the criminal justice system operates without ever addressing mechanisms of relegation, oppression, and domination. During a trial, the consequences of structural and collective forces are absent, even as, a few inches away, on the other side of the wall, their impact is visible for all to see.

When I began attending trials in the course of thinking about this book, the fact that I was defining my project in terms of sociology led me to think that I should explore at length the backstories and trajectories of defendants and victims and the social dynamics at work during a given proceeding: defendants' relationship to the official (French) language and to legal categories; the contrast between the social backgrounds of defendants, judges, and lawyers; and the varying ways in which individuals are treated according to social and ethnic background, gender, and so forth. I realized very quickly, however, that this approach wasn't necessary. First, because this method of analysis, intended to be critical, is inherent in the official definition of *sociology*, it is both expected and already accepted as valid. Everyone would have granted me the argument or

---

* Paris's Cours d'Assises. In France a *cour d'assisses* also refers to a jury court or assize court, which tries the most serious felonies before three judges and a six- or nine-person jury.—Trans.

premise that I would have ultimately produced, one that is already widely expressed, known, and understood. But also, and notably, I don't think there is any point in attempting to once again prove the value of a sociological perspective. Theories of justice, law, or delinquency no longer need to attempt to highlight the extent to which social drivers influence everything that each one of us—and therefore all those who become "criminals"—says and does. It goes without saying. Neither sociology nor social theory has to be on the defensive.

We therefore need to redefine the questions raised obligatorily by any modern analysis of the criminal justice system, which should focus on what can be called the mechanisms of denial. Our investigation should be centered on the penal state's propensity to deny reality and treat individuals as if social logics do not exist. Simply put, we must question the foundations, the violence, the political rationale, and the power effects of this practice of obscuring the social world.

NUMBERS

The acts and exchanges I witnessed during the years spent writing this book are merely one aspect of the practice of punitive criminal justice, or what I call the system of judgment and punishment. Day after day, week after week, an immense array of legal and repressive operations occurs in courtrooms, these spaces that are at once central, open, and—because they are so intimidating—little known. Individuals are placed in the dock: they are asked questions; they are interrogated; they hear testimony from experts, friends, acquaintances, victims, and psychologists and psychiatrists; they are reinterrogated, confronted. Next, two or three people argue against or on behalf of the defendant, who then waits, surrounded by police officers or gendarmes, for the court to finish deliberating and to reconvene. The court then announces whether it has decided to send the accused to prison or, very rarely, to release or acquit him or her. (France's national acquittal rate ranges between 7 and 10 percent, and I witnessed only one acquittal during my investigations.)

The justice system functions as an objective possibility in our lives that each of us must take into account and that shapes each one of us as a result. "None of us is sure to escape prison," stated the Groupe d'information sur les prisons (GIP) in its 1971 manifesto.[2] None of us is sure to escape justice either; indeed, none of us do. It is a part of our everyday lives. Rare are those individuals who will never find themselves facing a judge or lawyer, the threat of a prison sentence or damages, or the eventuality of pressing charges or being sued. But even those who never have any direct contact with the justice system will have been nonetheless unavoidably forced to take into account its existence and demands—the potential to be accused and/or convicted of a crime—if only precisely to avoid it, either by respecting the law or by adopting strategies of concealment.

The primary aim of this book is to question a reality whose validity we accept all too easily: the system of judgment and punishment. This doesn't mean simply observing and studying trials as they take place but rather using those observations to reconstruct the foundations of the criminal justice system on a broader scale and to identify the categories, perspectives, and narratives being instituted and reproduced.

When I speak of the system of judgment and punishment, I refer to an unconscious structure within which and based on which different national judicial systems define themselves and express their unique characteristics. In the same way that we can challenge

---

2. Michel Foucault, "Manifesto of the Group d'information sur les prisons (1971)," trans. Stuart Elden, *Viewpoint Magazine*, Feb. 16, 2016.

the very form of the prison, asylum, or camp, this book calls into question the trial and the court. What does the establishment of a criminal justice system and a punitive apparatus signify in a given society? What does it mean to judge and punish? To be judged? To accuse and to be accused? On what principles are these mechanisms based? What kinds of power, coercion, and domination do they exert? How does the criminal justice system manage the suffering or infliction of pain to which it gives rise?

My goal is to show the degree to which the modes through which the criminal justice apparatus is deployed are situated within a larger system of powers and perceptions. The functioning of justice in a society is intrinsically linked to other frameworks that organize social life, be they material or symbolic. Consequently, a study of the justice system cannot be limited to a local scale. On the contrary, we must endeavor to understand this system as the setting in which a broader, more global political rationale emerges and develops.

FOUNDATIONS

A close study of the theories and institutions of criminal justice is all the more necessary given that the institution of justice itself is constructed on foundations that have practically never been exhumed or questioned. A multitude of acts occur on a daily basis: people are judged, convicted or acquitted, or compensated. But in a way, the very repetition of those acts immunizes the penal apparatus from criticism. The system operates within the comfort of habit, an obvious and automatic way of reacting to illegal activity, unhindered by the need or desire to question what is happening. Accusing, summoning, judging, asking questions, and sentencing are all established rituals performed by a society without mastery of their meaning or logic. Paradoxically, that repetition doesn't produce a need to better understand or problematize the acts in question; instead, they become routine, positioned outside the domain of what can be challenged or deconstructed. This system's motives may well be hidden, but they continue to act unbeknownst to and in spite of us—and from that perspective we are governed by them.

During the trials I attended, there was always one moment that struck me as indicative of the justice system's capacity to run on empty, so to speak, without examining its own operations: the moment when the prosecution discusses the defendant's sentence. This moment, so revelatory of the mysterious nature of any criminal justice system, is akin to ritual, social magic. But nobody seems to notice its arbitrariness because, in reality, isn't this merely the transformation of a crime into time and money? A robbery garners X number of years and/or such-and-such a fine; a rape, X number of years; a murder, X number of years; and so forth.

Every criminal justice system differs when it comes to how and when this conversion of crime into time or money is discussed. In some countries it takes place during a separate hearing held after a guilty verdict is issued. In France the defendant's possible guilt is addressed at the same time as his sentence. At the end of the trial the prosecutor stands up and makes his case. He addresses the court (a panel of three judges and a jury) and first takes a position on the defendant's guilt. He then calls for conviction and states the punishment desired by the prosecution. But the length of imprisonment demanded often appears abrupt and without justification (supposing that such justification is possible).

Of course, the prosecutor never fails to add that the sentence must take into account the defendant's personality, the seriousness of the offense, and the harm to the victims. But these quasi-obligatory formulas are quickly followed by a recommendation, which lacks any visible logical or intelligible link between those considerations and the punishment: "You will sentence Mr. X to 12 years in prison," or, more often: "You will not sentence him to less than X years in prison."

In her book *La Vie ordinaire des assises* (The everyday life of the court), which describes eight trials observed by the author, Marie-Pierre Courtellemont recounts several of those surprising moments. She reproduces, for example, the closing speech delivered by the prosecution during a trial of two men accused of robbery held at the assizes court of Versailles. After attempting to establish the defendants' guilt, the prosecutor shifts focus to their personalities: "Are they easily influenced? I don't think so. Because if someone had told them 'let's jump off a bridge,' they would have refused. So why won't they give the names of their accomplices? I can only take that as a sign of recidivism. The law of silence is a code of honor in their world. Saint-Exupéry said: 'What is essential is invisible to the eye.' But for these men, the essential is what can be seen: clothes, cars, but definitely not other people, or respect for others."[3] And in a sequence typical of all the trials I was able to attend, the prosecutor moved without transition from these declarations to his recommendations: "I *therefore* call for 7 years of prison for K.A. and N.Y."[4]

Therefore? Why *therefore*? What is the relationship between the preceding statements and the called-for sentence? To what connection does *therefore* refer? What does it underscore, and to what does it draw attention if not, in the end, the impossibility of establishing any such connection?

Granted, on occasion prosecutors try to justify the sentences they recommend. But they do so exclusively by referencing custom, what is "habitual," in other words a scale of punishments instituted

---

3. Marie-Pierre Courtellemont, *La Vie ordinaire des assises* (Paris: Ramsay, 2005), 206.
4. Ibid.

in a given jurisdiction: in Paris, armed robbery warrants eight to ten years; manslaughter X years, etc. If you condemn the defendant to less or more time, the jury is told, you'll be challenging the "sentencing guidelines" and the exercise of justice, as well as the hierarchy between criminal courts and jury courts.* In short, punishments are considered solely according to a self-referential scale. The only justification that this institution can offer is expressed in terms of habit and tradition—"This is how it's done." A rational argument for the recommended sentence is never given, not that its absence prevents the justice system from handing down convictions on a daily basis. How strange that tradition be justified with tradition and, what's more, that we settle for such a justification! Especially when dealing with a system that, by its nature, has dramatic and concrete consequences on the lives of tens of thousands of people each year.

We cannot live in a penal state and accept governance by its laws, with all the implied consequences, without critically examining the system of judgment and the operations it conducts on us. The state power that is de facto exercised on our lives, liberty, and property is so intense that challenging it with radical and ethical concerns becomes a quasi-ontological necessity. We must put the state itself on trial and demand that the forces exerted on us be built on a rational, justifiable, and intelligible logic.

Taking a critical distance from the system of judgment entails, as for all other social institutions, suspending our belief in its inherent validity. At that point, challenging the penal state and the concepts, procedures, rituals, or functions associated with it, as well as the impulses driving it, may seem strange, pointless, naive, or foolish. Indeed, it's difficult to see the purpose of such an endeavor

---

* In France jury courts, or "*cours d'assisses,*" handle felonies, whereas criminal courts, or "*tribunaux correctionnels,*" are limited to misdemeanors.—Trans.

when, after all, "people should be judged for their actions," and it's hard to imagine the creation of a "system of impunity." How can we possibly avoid the existence of a legal system when punishments are intended to discourage crimes or reduce recidivism? What's the point of questioning the foundations of the criminal justice system when dismantling it would only increase violence and render the world unlivable?

This book is in no way intended to advance something that resembles, either directly or indirectly, suppression of the law or of the ethical order. That kind of objective would have zero meaning, interest, or pertinence. This also means that any such objections in that vein will be of no value. But I do want to reverse our perspective. I am struck by the fact that critical theory dedicates a great deal of its energy to imagining new arrangements that will redefine the global organization of our societies. Countless initiatives have proposed radical transformations of our world, calling into question national borders, economic structures, capitalism, democratic systems, the ecosystem, and the like. Yet it's difficult to find texts that critically examine the judicial apparatus and concepts of guilt, responsibility, sentencing, and punishment. The existing forms of the trial and act of judgment remain uncontested and appear incontestable, as if transforming the way we handle crimes and questioning our impulse to judge and punish appeared more utopian and out of reach than dismantling national borders or establishing communism on an international scale.

What is the source of the immunity of our system of judgment and the trial form? What intimate part of us does that system affect? And why are we so reticent to analyze it rationally?

SUBJECTS OF THE LAW
A REPRESSIVE THEORY OF POWER

Any study of the criminal justice system, the act of judgment, and associated concepts and procedures leads invariably to broader questions. Justice both symbolizes and guarantees the efficacy of state-imposed constraints. It ensures the functioning of the institution of law and the relationships between subjects of the law. The courtroom, in which an individual appears before a judge or judges, is a magnifying glass of our inscription within the legal order and our submission to its authority. The question of the penal state cannot therefore be reduced to the single, specific problem of managing illegal activity. Rather, it is our status as legal and political subjects that is at stake. How should we consider the fact that we are subject to the law? What does it mean to live under a rule of law? How can we understand the power effects exercised by the juridico-political order, and how do they function?

Ever since Michel Foucault's analyses in *The Will to Knowledge*, a large segment of critical thought has viewed power as a performative and constituent force, that is, a "positive" authority that produces the ways in which we live and act in the world. Many contemporary studies rely on the idea that considerations of power entail reconstructing the "subjectivities" and "identities" that it forms: the *Homo œconomicus*, the "neoliberal subject," the *Homo criminalis*, sexual- or gender-based identities, and the like.

When applied to the state, these modes of analysis lead us to believe that the legal order cannot be reduced to a set of constraints acting on each of us externally. Instead, the law fundamentally shapes how we are formed as subjects, how we relate to ourselves, and therefore how we behave; in other words, reflexivity, the way we perceive ourselves, will always already have been mediated by legal norms. Viewed from this perspective, the justice system doesn't impose obstacles or constraints on a previously formed subject. The subject is created *inside* the legal system and through its operations. In fact, legal rationality is what prompted the subject's emergence in the first place.

This view of the workings of the law has been taken up by philosophy with some regularity—in texts intended to be critical or not—in the work of Hegel, for example, but also in that of Walter Benjamin. Understanding our relationship to the law would therefore entail undertaking a genealogy of the responsible subject and analyzing this subjectification of self and resulting relationships with the world, as well as the kinds of experiences of which we are consequently dispossessed.

These ideas are clearly worthy ones and quite interesting. I myself used them in my book *The Art of Revolt* to defend the argument that Snowden, Assange, and Manning are inventing disruptive lifestyles that threaten the forms of subjectification that we experience as subjects under a rule of law. There, I suggest viewing these three unique individuals as "counter-subjects" who revolt against established political modes and thereby reveal the way that we are formed as "citizens" in liberal democracies.

So I understand the relevance of this view and am not claiming it to be necessarily false or incorrect. Its validity no doubt depends on the object of study, contexts, concerns, and what one wants to say or emphasize. Here, however, I propose approaching the question of power and violence differently. I'd like to take a step back from the performative theory of law. I'd also like to explain why I believe it is more relevant to evaluate our relationship with the forces acting on us in terms of repression when seeking to understand how the criminal justice apparatus and system of judgment function. In the world of theory we are too often inclined to adhere to the idea of performativity and to present powers as constituent forces. But that position prevents us from grasping the way the rule of law functions and, above all, the kind of violence it exerts.

Of course, it's not wrong to say that laws are performative statements, in the sense that their pronouncement and eventual application have a concrete impact on our lives. But the law doesn't only enact norms intended to guide and control behaviors: it is anchored to a figure of the subject and to a theory of action. It apprehends, redefines, and qualifies reality using its own categories. Trials are instances where we can observe the repressive state apparatus as it constructs narratives according to a highly specific interpretive framework: notions of responsibility, subject, intent, public order, damages, motives, victims, and complicity serve as instruments through which the law appropriates and interprets our actions and existences—to the detriment of other possible modes of restitution. Justice judges one representation of what we've done and our reasons for doing so. But that narrative is created based on a logic (a conception of conscience, will, interactions, and society) that conflicts with the reality that social analysis allows us to recreate. Part of the violence of the justice system comes from the fact that the penal state governs us by forcing us to correspond to an image of the subject that is *at odds with our true mode of existence*. It is this disconnect that causes and encapsulates the violence of the juridical order. In fact, that disconnect is itself violent. Being a subject of the law means being subjected to and confronted by the state's construction of reality and having to *live with it*. As a result the legal subject experiences a certain amount of dispossession and vulnerability.

The interesting question here is not our creation as subjects of the law but precisely the fact that we are not, *in reality*, subjects of the law. A critique of the state shouldn't begin with the subjectivities the state may produce but with the gap between what the state makes of us and what we really are, the difference between legal logics and those that are actually operative in the social world.

PUNISHMENT

My suggested approach to power is notably inspired by, and expands on, that put forth by Gilles Deleuze and Félix Guattari in *Anti-Oedipus*. In that work the two authors formulate a radical critique of psychoanalysis by exploring analytical practices and rereading texts by Sigmund Freud and Melanie Klein. They note an obsession with the figure of Oedipus and the family triangle within the field of psychoanalysis, in which everything appears to suggest that desires and impulses ultimately derive from a fixation on the figure of the mother or the father. But, to my mind, the most essential element of their argument is that in criticizing psychoanalysis and its influence, Deleuze and Guattari in no way maintain that its practices remake us in its image. The problem with psychoanalysis is not that it makes us into Oedipal subjects whose unconscious minds are entirely shaped by familial dynamics. On the contrary, Deleuze and Guattari insist on the existence of a gap—

an ontological difference—between the true way in which desire functions and the framework that psychoanalysis applies to it:

> Wouldn't the real difference be between Oedipus, structural as well as imaginary, and something else that all the Oedipuses crush and repress: desiring-production—the machines of desire that no longer allow themselves to be reduced to the structure any more than to persons, and that constitute the Real in itself, beyond or beneath the Symbolic as well as the Imaginary? . . . We even believe what we are told when Oedipus is presented as a kind of invariant. But the question is altogether different: *is there an equivalence between the productions of the unconscious and this invariant*—between the desiring-machines and the Oedipal structure? Or rather, does not the invariant merely express the history of a long mistake, throughout all its variations and modalities; the strain of an endless repression?[1]

The analysis offered by Deleuze and Guattari states essentially that psychoanalysis claims to understand our desires but does so with inadequate tools that don't match the reality of instinctual life. This inadequacy condemns psychoanalysis to producing effects of violence and mutilation. In short, the history of repression is the history of a mistake.

I employ a similar logic here. A critical approach must be linked to reality and the practice of truth. In other words, a social analysis of the penal state can't be limited to the descriptive—and supposedly neutral—task of understanding how it functions. Instead, we must highlight the gap between what sociology tells us (about ourselves, the world, and the logic of our actions) and the way in

---

1. Gilles Deleuze and Félix Guattari, *Anti-Oedipus: Capitalism and Schizophrenia*, trans. Robert Hurley, Mark Seem, and Helen R. Lane (Minneapolis: University of Minnesota Press, 1983), 52–53 (emphasis added).

which the system of judgment and punishment acts on us according to a different theory of action and the subject. We must confront the way in which the state treats reality with what we know from sociology. This means conducting a social analysis of the state, not in terms of understanding it but rather by using sociological reasoning to simultaneously challenge the validity of the frameworks imposed by the criminal justice system and to reveal their repressive nature.

FROM LAW TO CRITIQUE

The social theory–based analysis I develop is intended to identify the effects of power, order, and domination produced by social frameworks and, notably, in this work, legal and state frameworks. My aim is to revive what we might call a more resistant attitude toward the state. I'd like to use sociology as an instrument to reveal the hold that legal-political apparatuses have over us. This book is thus intended to restore the anti-institutional and destabilizing force of the social sciences. As the reader will see, the result will allow us to narrow the distance between the reasoning employed in social theory and the currents that have at times been set, wrongly, in opposition to it, such as left-libertarian (*libertaires*) approaches.*

That being said, I also want to clarify the complex way in which the problematic of the state and the law should be tackled

---

* The French word *libertaire*, which the author uses in the original, refers to an antiauthoritarian, individualist, and nonviolent leftist tradition of critiquing power and institutions that calls for the practices of equality and social justice. It is a term that would apply, for instance, to the political positions of figures like Pierre Bourdieu, whose influence is felt here, or Gilles Deleuze. Throughout this book the author and I have chosen to speak of left-libertarianism despite the potential inaccurate connotations of the word *libertarian* in English.—Trans.

from a critical perspective. My approach is in no way antistatist, as if the law were a negative, harmful, and coercive body that must be dismantled for us to become less "repressed" or more "free."

First of all, I am fully aware that violence exists outside of the state. I am by no means maintaining that the state constitutes the sole or even principal source of violence or that, by extension, there is any practical or theoretical validity to an approach that aims to abolish state-created frameworks. It's obvious that a state built on the rule of law, and that has established the rights of the accused and a system of appeals, represents progress and protection with respect to nonregulated structures of crimes and punishments (cycles of revenge, authoritarian states, etc.). The aspirations of populations deprived of the rule of law to build liberal criminal justice systems that reject arbitrary structures and the law of the jungle are not only comprehensible but also entirely legitimate.

However, being aware of those dimensions doesn't prevent us from conducting a critical analysis of the rule of law and the criminal justice system. In fact, that awareness may make such a project even more indispensable. If it is indeed true that the law justifies itself with its ambition to incarnate a rational order that is the least arbitrary possible, and that it is even intended to bring about a general reduction in the amount of violence, then it is only natural to evaluate the state's compliance with its own pretentions. In fact, I think it necessary to conduct a critical analysis of the law and the state in the name of the very values brandished by the latter. This entails evaluating to what extent legal mechanisms truly protect us from violence and determining if, on the contrary, they involuntarily provoke it in turn. When analyzing a system that aims to reduce violence, we must evaluate and diagnose state frameworks by asking the following questions: Do they really halt the cycle of violence, or do they also represent, in a way, a violent reaction to violence that is applied in the name of reason and law? And if that is the case, how can we envisage a more rational way of designing a system of judgment?

Another reason that formulating a critique of justice, left-libertarian or otherwise, doesn't equate to adopting an antistatist position is that the criminal justice system doesn't represent the entirety of the state; it's merely one of its dimensions. For that matter, it's only one aspect of the law as well. The state also encompasses the social state, social security, redistribution, the national education system, and even labor rights. As a result, it's entirely possible to attack, both theoretically and in practice, one state rationale or logic without attacking the entire structure. In other words, we can criticize the penal state, and even apply left-libertarian analytical principles to our investigation of the repressive judicial apparatus, without adopting an antistatist position from a fundamental and global perspective. Tensions and even contradictions are present within the state. It is therefore possible to challenge one of its many facets even while valorizing its other dimensions, much as Pierre Bourdieu did when comparing the "left and right hands of the state."* We can critique one state action by citing values that drive certain other actions, thereby challenging the state from the inside instead of the outside. Here, then, is a sort of state-based criticism of the state or, in any case, a critique that plays one conception of the state against another.

We can go even further and assert the essentially conservative—meaning unfounded—nature of all rhetoric that labels left-libertarian critiques of the state "anarchistic." I believe that any exercise that continuously and increasingly more meticulously ques-

---

* See Pierre Bourdieu, *Acts of Resistance: Against the New Myths of Our Time* (Cambridge: Polity, 1998).—Trans.

tions the functioning of the judicial order and its foundations is not only legitimate but *faithful to the spirit of the law and the state.*

After all, the state isn't an immutable substance that obligatorily displays this or that characteristic. Certain frameworks that define the state at a given moment can be dismantled or demolished, or they may simply disappear, to be replaced by others. The state is not composed of one given thing but is a political construction subject to transformation and choice. What characterizes the state at one moment can cease to do so in the next, even as measures that don't characterize it can subsequently emerge. In other words, criticizing the state system of penality can mean advocating that certain practices cease and, conversely, that the state adopt other rules and other practices. There is therefore no truth to the naive or absurd arguments that attempt to discredit left-libertarian critiques of the state by acting as if they can be reduced to an implicit celebration of anarchy. Criticizing the state always entails questioning those characteristics that apply to it during a specific period—and, at the same time, asking whether a different state or, at least, a transformation of the existing state is desirable or possible.

A critique of the law must never forget the idiosyncrasy and strength of the legal system—its ability to invent, renew, and transform itself. The state and the law represent, in a sense, a world of invention, experimentation, and creation—of historicity, in other words. With the law it is always possible to construct a new and more rational, valid, and livable world. This means that, in principle, there is no reason to limit ourselves when reflecting on the law.

An analysis of justice must therefore explore to what extent sociology, ethical concerns, and left-libertarian or pluralist values can serve as the point of departure for imagining other mechanisms and for teaching us to perceive crime, causality, and responsibility differently so as to construct other narratives of events that introduce more rationality and less violence, more freedom and less punishment. Is it possible to imagine another form of the criminal justice system? What are the limits and lacunas of existing mechanisms?

Reforms of judicial procedure, the rights of the accused, the role of victims, and other forms of punishment are no doubt regularly taken into consideration. Yet the transformation of certain key concepts of the judicial system appears, on the contrary, to represent a quasi-unattainable task. But the establishment of legal mechanisms that are new or at least different from those we believe to be unsurpassable is not pure speculation or wishful thinking. Redefining justice—conceptions of the courtroom, sentencing, responsibility, and repression—based on political, ethical, and critical concerns isn't an unprecedented endeavor. *It already exists and has existed for some time.* This can be demonstrated notably by the analysis of "transitional justice," meaning mechanisms of justice put into place after a civil war or a revolution, such as the Truth and Reconciliation Commission in South Africa, the International Criminal Tribunal for Rwanda, or the Commission for Reception, Truth, and Reconciliation in East Timor. A study of those procedures reveals the extent to which the need to consider justice (and thus crime, guilt, and punishment) in relation to political, historical, and ethical considerations (establishing civil peace after a conflict, consolidating a democratic regime, etc.) has led to the establishment of new relationships with justice and new kinds of trials that approach and construct notions of responsibility, punishment, judges' neutrality, evidence, and related matters differently. Who should be judged after the collapse of a repressive regime and for which crimes? How far down—to which rank—should we "descend" in the chain of responsibility? Should everyone be judged? And what meaning can the punishment of one individual, even a long prison term, have in relation to the suffering of thousands of victims? Doesn't an overly harsh and automatic punishment risk unleashing another civil war instead of interrupting the cycle of violence?

"Transitional justice" is the name of a form of penal justice—or, to be more precise, it may no longer be strictly "penal"—that is inventive, audacious, and different. At times it favors reconciliation and the determination of truth over punishment. This form of justice doesn't necessarily seek to reprimand, punish, or imprison the guilty. It also occasionally breaks with impersonal procedures and the neutrality of judges in order to foster in them a sense of empathy for the victims, thus allowing the latter to express their emotions. In her book *La Justice transitionnelle* (Transitional justice), Kora Andrieu writes, for example:

> Transitional justice, in all its forms, accords a very large place to emotion. It essentially establishes a staging of the crime whose point is narrative rather than punitive: thus truth commissions established in South Africa, Chile, Morocco, or Argentina were primarily intended to establish the facts rather than condemn the guilty, and to offer the victims an arena in which they could finally express their suffering and see it publicly acknowledged. The legitimization of this method is intrinsically psychological and moral: the narration of facts is intended to appease the victims' suffering ("talk therapy") at the same time that it subjects the torturers to public opprobrium ("naming and shaming"). In fact, amnesty of the guilty parties, granted in the name of the reconciliation of the community of survivors and the rebuilding of the nation, is very often part of transitional justice policies. This is not, however, considered to be equivalent to amnesia or total impunity:

the demonstration and narration of horrors are considered to be more noble and ethical forms of justice. Forgiveness becomes the supreme form of what is just.[1]

I don't agree with the entirety of Andrieu's statements or identify with her theoretical framework—far from it. Her book remains captive to a classical political liberalism that is quite conservative (for example, not overly acknowledging "differences" so as to preserve "a world in common"). It is also colored by a vocabulary of reconciliation and need for recognition of which I am wary. But that aspect is secondary here. More important is the fact that, by linking the question of justice to concerns either political (the end of a war, the establishment of democracy) or ethical (victims' suffering, the meaning of responsibility in an authoritarian regime), it was possible to put into place unprecedented mechanisms that codified what it means to dispense justice in a new way.

Transitional justice is in no way a model for me; I don't believe this type of judicial procedure should "replace" the existing criminal justice system. For that matter, transitional justice, which has taken on very different forms in various times and places, can't be used to create one uniform "model." But it does offer proof that another form of justice is possible, that another criminal justice system can be envisaged, and that notions of responsibility, penality, crime, and punishment can be redefined and redeveloped. History isn't over yet. We can't accept the current forms and modes of the system of judgment as self-evident and irreproachable. There is no reason to think that the structure of our justice system rep-

---

1. Kora Andrieu, *La Justice transitionnelle* (Paris: Gallimard, 2012), 38–39. In *La Justice en procès* Jean Bérard pieces together various militant traditions critical of the criminal justice system that developed in the wake of May '68. See Jean Bérard, *La Justice en procès* (Paris: Presses de Sciences-Po, 2013).

resents the culmination of all possibilities. In short, liberating our imaginations—expanding the way in which we conceive of justice and the law—is an entirely legitimate undertaking.

PART TWO
THE STATE AND VIOLENCE

CIVILIZATION AND ITS LIES

I've always had a marked, and doubtless banal, interest in courtrooms. I wouldn't describe it as an obsession, or a "fascination," to borrow the term used by André Gide to describe his relationship to justice in his *Recollections of the Assize Court*. My attraction to these places has instead been nourished by the feeling that something rather unusual occurs there. The judicial machine has always struck me as an extraordinary institution but not so much because of the stories or the tragedies recounted therein. The intriguing nature of the courtroom as a site of power (which explains the "fascination" it can hold) is more rooted, in my opinion, in the fact that it reveals our condition as subjects of the state, allowing us to experience tangibly something that, ultimately, we have trouble conceptualizing and whose intensity we rarely measure: the fact that we belong to the state. The time, energy, and resources that the state dedicates to identifying, questioning, and punishing individuals who have allegedly broken the law; the acceptance of and submission to the judicial apparatus; the irresolvability or incertitude to which court proceedings lead; the random nature of judgments and the extraordinary consequences to which they lead; the incomprehension, anger, or resignation provoked by verdicts—all this makes for a scene that itself encapsulates what it means to live in a state: the intermingling of the logics of protection, dispossession, submission, and vulnerability that characterize our existence as individuals answerable to the law, which is to say, both at the state's disposal and in its hands.

My interest in the justice system has led me to regularly—indeed, as often as possible—read everything that has to do with the law and that depicts trials, judges, lawyers, and defendants: newspaper articles, court transcripts, academic essays and studies, news programs, films, documentaries, and novels. These kinds of productions, and the narratives they disseminate, were at the forefront of my mind when I began attending court proceedings in preparation for writing this book.

Yet, from the first trial I attended, nothing went as I expected. I was immediately struck by the extent to which prevailing images of justice, to which I myself had been exposed, were false—or, rather, distorted. There is a startling disparity between cultural representations of the courtroom and its reality. This means that the first question any analysis of the justice system must address is that of images of the state, and by extension of language, and of the possibility of constructing narratives that show the state for what it actually is and that challenge misleading ones.

MYTHS OF THE COURTROOM

Cultural representations of the courtroom traditionally depict trials as charged and intense. Take, for example, the use of the metaphor of the spectacle: the trial is described or shown as a theater where a "drama" unfolds, replete with intrigues, plot twists, suspense, and indecision that culminates in the climactic moment of the verdict. This kind of staging constructs the trial as a ceremony in which each silence or pause, each minute that goes by, and every word spoken is filled with tension, anxiety, and intensity. The criminal courtroom is like a tragedy whose lead players are the lawyers, defendants, witnesses, and judges.

There is another mystifying way to describe trials, one that relies more on a religious or majestic vocabulary than one of performance. It is the metaphor of ritual, whereby justice is transformed into a rite and the trial a solemn moment during which the state publicly displays its strength and authority. Here, the trial appears as a kind of institution intended to impress and establish the transcendent nature of the state, law, and juridical order—all to inspire respect and obedience.

It suffices to attend a trial to realize the falseness of these representations. The metaphors of the theatrical drama and the religious ceremony that saturate symbolic representations of the courtroom— be they movies, plays, or articles and essays about the law—aren't instruments that can be used to reveal or get closer to a certain truth. They are discursive elements that create a gap between perception and reality. Trials have none of the intense, solemn, spectacular, or impressive moments to which we are so often treated. On the contrary, they are full of the dull, the undramatic, and the routine. Proceedings unfold calmly, evenly, and quasi-mechanically—in short, normally.

Each time I visited a courtroom in Paris, I was overcome by a feeling of disappointment and dismay. This was because nothing struck me as noteworthy. Nothing extraordinary or even merely interesting was going on. Everything during the trial—the questions asked by lawyers and the court, the responses given by witnesses and defendants, the speeches made by lawyers and prosecutors, and often even the verdicts and sentences—unfolded in a linear manner: no surprises, no spectacle, no emotion, and no violence.

Direct examinations, expert testimonies, and the circulation of photos were monotonous. Arguments weren't at all engaging but dragged on and got bogged down in unimportant details. Nor were they grandiose. The whole process was akin to a bureaucratic and mundane procedure, filled with improvisations, errors, and dead time. Indeed, the emotion that I most consistently experienced and that best describes my feelings throughout the trials that I observed (and that has stayed with me) was boredom. I now wonder how it is possible to think of trials as imposing affairs.

POWER COMES FROM BELOW

The disparity between established representations of the courtroom and its reality might appear anecdotal and secondary. One might be tempted, as is often done in purportedly scholarly works, to simply qualify public images of justice as false and dismiss them before directly proceeding to the description of the true reality.

But such an approach would sidestep an important issue. Put another way, we have to take seriously the disparity between representation and truth; it constitutes an avenue through which we can question our culture, our perceptions, and our relationship to the state. Furthermore, this gap paves the way for a critical investigation of images of reality, perception, and the logics of subjugation and sovereignty. Why does culture propagate a mystifying image of the state? What function does that image serve? How should we understand this lie that culture creates—or, better yet, the fundamentally deceptive nature of culture itself?

Theories of politics and domination have shown that there is a relationship between power and images. Historians and sociologists have pieced together the way in which state domination relies on the construction, circulation, or imposition of a number of myths, narratives, or apparatuses intended to produce gratitude, obedience, and submission. A symbolic economy of power exists in which political authority counts on representations to legitimize itself.

But, however established that mechanism may be, my own experience, which I recount here, was completely different. Even if we can correctly maintain that the state often produces myths aimed at imposing and legitimizing its authority, the belief in its grandiose nature seems, bizarrely, to *come from ourselves*. By all appearances, the producers of cultural goods—journalists, intellectuals, filmmakers, directors, artists—project a solemnity and a ritualistic character onto the courtroom that it doesn't claim for itself.

It suffices to visit a place in which the state exerts its power to experience concretely this absence of majesty. Nothing takes on an impressive character. In other words, the state does not force an awe-inspiring representation of sites of power upon us. Rather, it is we who appear to be attached to that representation, we who create and perpetuate it, even as the truth remains in plain sight.

The metaphors through which the courtroom is understood should therefore not merely be "deconstructed." These images should also be denounced as falsifying rhetoric and mystifications. They function as institutional facades. Culture—films, plays, and books—creates subjugating artifacts that distort the concrete functioning of activities *that the state itself doesn't hide*. These are therefore not innocent fictions but political ones that elevate the state high above us—and that betray a passion for sovereignty.

Indeed, one might wonder whether the logic of power isn't fundamentally tied to a kind of drive for sovereignty. If it is, we are dealing with the issue of political alienation, in which individuals' perceptions of themselves and their ontological status hinge on the grandeur of the state to which they belong: raise up the state to raise up oneself, to feel as if one belongs to something grand. In *The Will to Knowledge* Foucault says that we need to cut off the king's head in order to establish a critical theory of power. I believe that, first off, we must stop pretending we can see the emperor's new clothes.

Art, literature, and cinema—true to life or not—like to think of themselves as critical domains that distance us from ourselves, creating spaces of resistance that allow us to feel momentarily free. But when it is a question of the state, the producers of symbolic goods appear to create subjugating fictions: they dress the state in clothes it doesn't actually wear, attributing it a solemnity that it in fact lacks; in short, they construct it as sovereign. It's as if there is a passion or urge driving these producers to use their creative faculties not to produce realistic visions or critical fiction but to safeguard false images whose sole aim is to accentuate processes of "solemnization" aimed at reinforcing attitudes of submission and obedience. This approach runs contrary to the critical method, which always strives to undermine sovereignty, to make it less impressive than it appears, and to thereby foster a resistance to "authorities."

Art and imagination are often associated with criticism because they incarnate a possibility of creating distance from reality and fostering the desire and need to transform it. Yet here, precisely for that reason, they appear complicit with forces of order, which rely on a logic of lies and mystifications. Conversely, sociological practice, happy to tell it like it is, so to speak, has a liberating effect. . . .

SEE THE STATE
FOR WHAT IT IS

The deconstruction of myths and mystifications is a slow and complex task that necessarily entails several stages. Everything can't be deconstructed in one go. It would be impossible to liberate ourselves from ideologies once and for all, and any critical endeavor must therefore tackle problems one at a time. It is entirely possible to challenge some mystifications with arguments that will themselves be deconstructed in turn.

This is why I want to explore whether formulating a lucid understanding of the operations of the state and the law requires a new rupture in the first place. Might not the act of observing a trial, and feeling as if it is unfolding in a serene and neutral fashion, be the very sign that one is prey to an illusion or, more precisely, a political impression shaped by a narrative that should be called into question?

What do we see when we take a seat in the gallery of a criminal court and assume the role of an observer who believes him- or herself impartial or a "field ethnologist": reality or a prefabricated image of reality forged by the state? Is the image of court proceedings as a series of calm and rational moments true? Or does it in fact reflect the official characterization of the criminal justice procedure as the very opposite of the logics of passion, war, vengeance, and backward rituals? Doesn't the reality we perceive and observe actually express an internalization of ideologies, notably, in this case, the legal ideology on which the modern state is founded in its legal-rational form, that is, the acceptance of its proffered definitions of violence and nonviolence—in short, a foregone conclusion that should be dismantled?

INFLICT PAIN

During these moments of doubt, confronted with these types of questions, we realize the importance of theory, of reflection, and of breaking with spontaneous modes of engagement with the world in order to detach ourselves and deconstruct our individual experiences. Ultimately, only by placing the world at a distance can we see the blind spots, lies, and illusions that shape our understanding of what is presented, at first glance, as reality. Once we become aware of these errors, we're almost ashamed to have not seen the truth sooner.

The famous article "Violence and the Word," by the American legal scholar Robert Cover, introduces just such a break. Cover transforms our understanding of the law, of grasping what happens during a trial, and therefore of problematizing justice and the state. He maintains that to analyze the judicial system, we must transform the way in which we spontaneously view it. We must break with modes of perception that tend to neutralize the apparatus of criminal justice. Cover notably targets legal scholars and political philosophers and the way in which they shape our view of the courts. Interpretations of legal decisions frequently employ categories like "lawmakers," "rationality," and "system." These interpreters place themselves in the role of the judge. They try to understand his or her verdict and the way in which his or her justifications reflect established doctrine and the system of norms meant to govern "social life." But this analytical mode results in bias. A legal decision is not, in fact, an argument whose validity and rationality should be verified. Nor is it a discourse that expresses or integrates collective and collectively shared norms within a democratic society. It is a localized act that targets someone, that fractures the world, that strikes down. Cover doesn't ask us to change our point of view. He doesn't tell us to stop looking at the law from the judge's perspective. He asserts that we need to change our way of conceptualizing and understanding what occurs in the courtroom whenever a judge speaks. What matters is not what the judge says but what he or she does. And what the judge does, objectively, is harm. *To judge is to inflict violence.* All legal interpretations inflict suffering on the individuals to whom they're applied, whether it be by imprisoning them, taking away their property, or killing them.[1]

When we think about justice, then, we must think about *a "practice" whose "objective" is to cause pain*. If we want to label what happens inside a courtroom, we must acknowledge that it generates violence.[2] In other words, constructing a transparent (read: nonmystifying) analysis of the justice system requires that we reject all language or frameworks that lead to its portrayal as a peaceful setting. Perceiving a trial as monotonous and dull or believing that the court is an institution in which proceedings take place dispassionately is an error, equivalent to *not seeing what is happening*. All the moments that we initially perceive to be calm, and all the acts that appear nonviolent because they are rational and bureaucratic,

---

1. See Robert M. Cover, "Violence and the Word," *Yale Law Journal* 95, no. 8 (1986): 1601–29.
2. Ibid., 1610. On suffering as knowledge and a learning process see Édouard Louis, "Savoir-Souffrir," in "Que peut (encore) la littérature?" ed. Stéphane Audeguy and Philippe Forest, La Nouvelle revue française, no. 609 (Oct. 2014): 123–34.

are in fact extremely intense: the operations of the law create antagonisms, divisions, and fractures through which the judge inflicts a constraint and an act of violence on the accused. *The courtroom becomes the scene of an assault.*

VIOLENCE:
A USEFUL CATEGORY OF ANALYSIS

Cover's vision reveals the value of the concept of violence as an analytical category that allows us to break with prevalent thinking about the law and state practices: the court's violent character doesn't appear exclusively, or perhaps even primarily, at specific moments—for example, during verbal exchanges or when guards take away the convicted defendant following the verdict. It doesn't intermittently erupt alongside calmer moments. There is a structural violence to the trial form that goes beyond individual interactions and that underlies the very nature of the legal order.

For that matter we can, in this regard, add another dimension to Cover's analysis and thus, in my opinion, embolden it. The violence of the criminal justice system doesn't stem solely from the fact that every legal act or decision has concrete consequences on an individual's life and person. It is also rooted in the fact that a trial must be understood as a moment of extreme dispossession. This situation, whose violent nature we don't automatically perceive, is aimed at placing individuals (not only defendants, on whom I concentrate in this section, but also victims, witnesses, and jurors) *at the disposition* of the state at all times. Incidentally, the expression "in the judge's hands" or "in the hands of the police" crops up repeatedly. The launch of a criminal procedure signifies that someone's life has been put on hold. His fate is no longer his own but is controlled by the state; judges and/or jurors will decide, according to their own criteria, what will become of him. After hearing from witnesses, his accusers, and his defense, they will withdraw, deliberate, and then deliver a verdict.

A court constitutes what I suggest we call a site of power—a space in which the meaning of being a subject of law materializes. My relationship to the state and the law is first and foremost one of imposition and obligation: I am born in a state and I am obliged to be its subject. I can neither break that bond nor escape it. I am subject to the order of law.

Of course, a critical analysis of the law should not be one-sided or binary. It is entirely accurate to say that the law can serve as a protective and liberating space. We cannot only consider the law as a system of constraints that impede individual action or the state as a negative, restrictive, and coercive body. Legal constraints can also be viewed as safeguards offered to all. Indeed, the existence of an abstract legal order has served regularly as an extremely powerful instrument used by marginalized groups in their fight for equality and emancipation.

But possession of these positive rights assumes first an act of inclusion through which the subject is established as belonging to the state, as a subject of the criminal justice system, meaning a subject to whom the criminal justice system applies. As subjects of the law we are all potential objects of criminal proceedings. Any person can be targeted by the police and the law at any moment; we are all vulnerable to investigation, detention, and judgment. The existence of criminal law goes hand in hand with that of a system through which the state assumes the right to dispose of an individual's fate: anyone can be arrested, locked up, and judged. Note that every year, tens of thousands of individuals are found not guilty of crimes of which they were accused—men and women on whom the legal and police machinery descended in an unjustified and arbitrary manner and who suffered physical, mental, and material consequences.

Those cases tell us something fundamental about who we are: we cannot view the justice system as an institution that doesn't concern us. It can strike us at any moment. We live in an ontological state of precarity, susceptible of being stopped by the state at any time because its various bodies assume the right to intervene in our lives and decide what to do with us according to their own logic. *Living under the rule of law means living in a context in which the state has the right to dispose of us.*

Contrary to what a large proportion of political theory maintains, *being a subject of the law does not mean, first of all, being a protected and secure subject. We are first and foremost subjects who can be judged—that is, imprisoned, arrested, and convicted.* We are vulnerable subjects, dispossessed in relation to the logic of the state. The protections offered by the criminal justice system presuppose inclusion in that very system. They even require our submission to it, as legal rights function according to modes and forms that are predetermined and codified by procedure. The court is perhaps the institution in which individuals' dispossession in relation to the state and their vulnerability in relation to the rule of law are the most intense. It's one of the rare arenas in the social world in which the state-appropriated right to control and decide the fate of individuals—citizens or otherwise—appears in its true guise. Within this site of power the state has the right to make decisions about an individual's life without ever requesting that the latter consent to submit to state authority or offering the possibility that she or he renounce the state altogether.

Here we find ourselves confronted with a system that eludes and serves as the exception to what Pierre Bourdieu called the social paradox of the logic of power, namely, that in order for someone else to exercise power over me, I need to give him or her the chance to do so; I must, in other words, play their game. I can only suffer the effects of the power exercised and be affected by its decisions if I engage with a given world, accord importance to what takes place within it, and acknowledge the value of its stakes. It's precisely because I believe in and adhere to the stakes of the internal struggles of a given field (what Bourdieu calls the *illusio*) that I'm subject to it—thereby ensuring that power always and necessarily operates with my complicity. If I don't believe in or commit to the stakes of a given field (be it cultural, scientific, sports-related, or what have you), I will ignore its dominant authorities and categories of judgment, and, as a result, the specific power won't apply to me—it will remain external to me and will not concern me.[3]

The legal and criminal justice system operates differently, however. The state forcibly brings me under its authority. The specificity of the state comes from the fact that it constitutes a power that strips its subjects of the possibility of renouncing it. The courtroom itself affirms publicly a phenomenon *that is iteratively renewed and reasserted each time a trial begins—the state's control over its subjects, the fact that we are at the state's disposition and can be summoned to appear before it.*

The kind of emotion I'm hoping to convey here is well conveyed in a documentary by Jean-Xavier de Lestrade entitled *The Staircase*. The film centers on the trial of a man accused of murdering his wife. Uncertainty and doubt about what happened, and the very ability to ever definitively know the truth, mount as the proceedings unfold. The trial goes on for several months, culminating in the moment when the jury is confined to a small, isolated, and guarded room, cut off from the outside world, to decide the verdict. Deliberations last a week, after which the jury returns to announce its decision. If found guilty, Michael Peterson will be au-

---

3. Pierre Bourdieu, *Méditations pascaliennes* (Paris: Seuil, 1997), 247–88.

tomatically sentenced to life in prison; if found not guilty, he will be acquitted and can go home.

What does it mean to be subjected to a system of such outrageous power? What does it mean to accept these circumstances and this mechanism? How can such an important decision be reached in a context of such vast uncertainty unless the state, in reality, actually does demonstrate its unpredictable and therefore sovereign nature in this way? The documentary's recreation of the waiting involved in a trial, followed by the moment when the verdict is announced, concretely, and almost physically, reveals the violence inherent in the justice system, our vulnerability to the state, the dispossession that comes with being at its disposition, and the fatalism (rather than rebellion) to which this situation leads.

THE DOUBLE REALITY
OF VIOLENCE

A trial is not a show. It isn't a ritual or a drama; it is not an awe-inspiring ceremony. But neither is it, as we may be initially inclined to believe, a peaceful, subdued way of dealing with illegal activity. A trial is one of the most intense apparatuses of social life: an individual watches his freedom, property, relationships, "reputation," sufferings, and, in certain countries, his life be subjected to decisions made by a third party. In both form and content analytical theory must rise to that situation. It should be guided by one essential concern: to reveal the reality, and not a euphemistic vision, of what's at stake and in so doing pave the way for critical thinking.

Telling the truth thus entails highlighting the fact that during a trial violence is everywhere; it is in every interaction, violence of procedure, violence of argument, of situation, of the law, and of dispossession. But this violence doesn't represent a gap or flaw in the rationalization and bureaucratization of this site of power. There is an inherent violence in legal-rational procedures that we must consider in order to understand what we are.

That said, a critical theory of the state cannot limit itself to revealing the state's violence or to identifying the ways in which that violence is exercised. If our thinking were to proceed in this way, we would be unable to grasp reality in its entirety, a reality that includes the way we experience it and that is itself characterized by a blindness (albeit partial) to the violence of the state. The violence of the court isn't immediately perceptible. We either don't see it at first glance, or we only glimpse it superficially and, in any case, not in its full intensity. The law and criminal procedure, operating according to their own specific modalities, inflict violence that *we do not perceive as such*. We need a theoretical approach that reflects on legal acts and on our condition as subjects of the law if we are to become fully conscious of the extent of this violence.

Our inability to immediately grasp the true workings of the state is neither self-evident nor obligatory. It stems from the fact that we've internalized images or ways of looking at the state that conceal its true workings. How can we explain the state's odd ability to make violent actions appear nonviolent, or the fact that we don't perceive those actions as they truly are? What paradigms are involved in this process of political blindness? What are the obstacles to establishing a lucid perception of the state? And, conversely, what conditions are necessary to formulate a critical theory of the relationships between the state and violence?

POLITICAL PHILOSOPHY

The first major obstacle to a satisfactory analysis of the state is political philosophy. There is a contradiction between an endeavor aimed at understanding the violence of the law and the perceptions constructed, imposed, and circulated by the tradition of political philosophy. In other words, we need to dismantle the established vocabulary of political thought if we wish to formulate a critical analysis of power.

The task that political philosophy has assigned itself can be defined as follows: imagine a way to describe the state without mentioning violence; ensure that our relationship to the law is neutralized; and offer a depoliticized perception of politics. It's striking, for example, to observe the extent to which notions of violence, force, and coercion are practically absent from texts like John Rawls's *A Theory of Justice*. Indeed, such a vocabulary appears to be completely foreign to the author.

This perspective, which is in the Kantian tradition and reappears in writings by Hannah Arendt and, more recently, Jürgen Habermas, presupposes that, at bottom, the state cannot be violent *as a matter of principle*.

The construction of a specific "political" sphere signifies the construction of an arena in which the law is developed through discussion, reasoning, and deliberation. Here, *law* is synonymous with *majority* (in other words, it is only in democracy that there is "law" worthy of its name). Political norms thus stem from procedures and rules that are formulated in accordance with logics of choice, reciprocity, or mutual recognition, such that these norms will be produced by the same individuals to whom they apply. The legal order aims to be universal, rational, and recognized. Application of the law may of course constitute a constraint and rely on a specific power. But those constraints and powers, which the subject recognizes as applicable to her or him as a citizen, are *nonviolent*.

Throughout the history of political philosophy, its impetus has consisted of grounding the law in processes presented as both rational and collective in order to guarantee its normative authority a kind of immunity from criticism. The idea is that if the law is based on collective reasoning, then the state is, in principle, *nonviolent*. The very idea of the state assumes that the state is nonviolent; when it acts in its official capacity, when it respects the procedures and rules on which it was founded or that it decreed, violence is theoretically impossible. Violence is arbitrary, associated with private, civil society—the very sphere against which the state positions itself as autonomous. Violence—vendettas, vengeance, and the like—predates the state or exists beyond it, in the private, civil world. By definition, violence is situated outside the law, such that any author who uses violence to define the state will find him- or herself accused of being incapable of conceptualizing the political sphere in its specificity. The state can only be described as violent if it betrays its principles—meaning precisely if it is dissolved as a state and stops acting in a legal way. In *Between Facts and Norms* Habermas takes on sociology, which he accuses of "undermining" the normativism of rational law by reducing it to nonlegal logics and the problematic of the state to one of domination. Sociology is presented as a discipline that analyzes the law as a form of imposition, not as a domain aimed at social integration through operations of mutual understanding carried out by communicating subjects. As a result, it bypasses the unique character of this sphere of action and discussion where politics and the law are constituted.[1]

This operation of fetishizing and promoting the state reaches its pinnacle in the distinction Hannah Arendt believes necessary between "power"—or "authority"—and "violence." She considers power to be the manifestation of a collective will developed through deliberative operations, whereas violence refers to instrumental mechanisms of domination, constraint, and imposition.[2] By linking politics and nonviolence, political theory attributes to the state an exceptional status. Within this framework the system of justice does not appear violent. Rather, it represents the appli-

---

1. Jürgen Habermas, *Between Facts and Norms: Contributions to a Discourse Theory of Law and Democracy*, trans. William Rehg (Cambridge, MA: MIT Press, 1996), 56.
2. Hannah Arendt, *Crises of the Republic* (San Diego: Harcourt Brace, 1972).

cation of a law based on discussion and collective agreement—a process that is recognized collectively as legal and has the right to be enforced. Like all citizens, the person being judged recognizes the legitimacy of the criminal procedure being applied to him or her because it incarnates the normal consequence, under a rule of law, of actions that run contrary to the law. From that perspective, being judged does not mean that violence is being exerted against me by the state; I am not being judged by an external power. The application of the criminal justice system represents my will as a rational and political being and demonstrates recognition of my status as a subject of the law.[3] I am not the one judging myself, but I am consenting to a system of judgment and am recognizing the legitimacy of an institution that may eventually punish me. This is what allows Kant, for example, to maintain that far from being a victim of violence, the subject condemned to death is in reality, at that moment, being treated and recognized by the state as a subject of the law—in other words, that he or she is enjoying an ontological promotion.

To problematize the question of the violence of the order of law, we must break with the rhetoric of political philosophy, a mode of analysis that tries to establish the foundations of the law while removing the question of violence. To do so, it invokes mystifying fictions (deliberation, representation, contract, democracy) destined to immediately incorporate us into the system of law and transform us into citizens who both desire and recognize said system. In other words, *the only possible critical theory of the state and violence* is one based on social theory, the sole discipline that represents the state as it is, compared to political philosophy, which operates as a tool of mystification.

---

3. See Frédéric Gros, "Les quatre foyers de la peine," in *Punir en démocratie* (Paris: Odile Jacob, 2001), 40.

POLITICAL SOCIOLOGY

A collective analysis of the state and violence represents one of the great victories of the social sciences. Whereas political philosophy aims to disconnect the idea of violence from the state by separating the sphere of civil or private interactions from the public sphere, historical and sociological models, notably Norbert Elias's classic essay "On the Monopoly Mechanism," insist on the question of coercion: constraint is viewed as essential to understanding the birth and perpetuation of the state. The state emerges from the monopolization of violence by a specific group that imposes itself as dominant and universal. The form it takes stems from the concentration of violence in one central organization and the corresponding dispossession of other social or economic actors' right to violence. The state establishes a military, policing, legal, and fiscal monopoly. It takes the right to enact violence away from other agents. Its dominance is therefore linked to both the unification and pacification of a given territory.

This description of the state as an authority that, by monopolizing violence, works to ensure the cohesion of a territory against anarchy, civil war, and constant sedition is an invaluable contribution. It represents a necessary point of departure that challenges the political vision of politics and the contractual or deliberative perception of the law by resituating the state inside a sphere of warring social institutions and by highlighting the arbitrary, contingent, and unique character of juridical mechanisms as well as their essential contribution to the consolidation of a given social and political order.

Despite this original intention behind a social science of the state, however, social and historical theory can also hinder reflections on violence—and actually, in their current form, they do just that. They tend not to conceptualize and problematize violence as such and in and of itself. This strange omission can first be explained by the fact that sociological and historical analyses are implicitly based on a narrative that depicts official violence as both secondary and necessary: the police and the justice system are meant solely to be *responses* to preceding violence. That response by *repressive* authorities—the adjective reveals the presupposed secondariness of state action in relation to forces that naturally emerge inside the social sphere—is meant to reestablish order and prevent private conflicts or perpetual cycles of vengeance from spreading. State violence is perceived as a counterviolence, or one form of violence against another, thanks to which peace, coexistence, and political unity are maintained in the face of war, anarchy, and political dissolution. While this, of course, remains a form of violence, it is a pacifying one. As a result, state violence isn't perceived or treated as debatable; nor is it viewed as a reality that can be criticized, transformed, or diminished. The ends of state violence are seen as self-evident, which shields it from criticism.

The paradoxical difficulty encountered by the social sciences in problematizing official violence is amplified by a second element: Max Weber's classic and prevailing definition of the state. This definition insists on the fact that we cannot accept the reductive view that the state uses violence in the same way as any other institution. It rejects the relevance of all frameworks that equate the state with rival private actors that evolve in the social world. The state is not an actor like the rest; the constraint it imposes is, in its case, recognized as legitimate. The state is an authority that successfully claims a monopoly of *legitimate* physical violence within a given territory.

This definition has followed a strange trajectory. It consists of two inseparable elements: violence and recognition. Yet it has prompted a quasi-exclusive focus on the question of legitimacy, while relegating violence to a position of secondary importance. According to this definition, the state's unique character comes from its subjects' acceptance of its coercive nature and their recognition of its legitimacy. As a result, the question of legitimacy has been framed as the fundamental problem in analyses of the state: How does a state legitimize its violence? Under what conditions is its coercion recognized, accepted, and interiorized, and why is it sometimes not? How are those crises of legitimacy essential to understanding political crises?

This rendering invisible of state violence can't be dismissed as a bad interpretation or transmission of Weber's text. Weber himself does the same thing. Let's examine, for example, his "Politics as a Vocation," in which he first seeks a way to define the state. He maintains that, from a sociological perspective, we can't define the modern state by its aims or objectives (since other nonstate groupings may have had similar goals over history). The modern state should thus be characterized by a "specific means peculiar to it"—"physical force," in other words. Weber cites Trotsky: "Every state is founded on force," and notes, "That is indeed right," before making his famous assertion: "A state is a human community that (successfully) claims the monopoly of the legitimate use of physical force within a given territory."[4]

Notions of domination, constraint, and violence occupy a central position in the definition of the modern state. Yet Weber will quickly eliminate them. They will be forgotten. Instead, Weber concentrates on another aspect: recognition of the legitimacy of violence. For the state to exist, "the dominated must obey the authority claimed by the powers that be." Hence the questions that dominate his analysis: When and why do men obey? How do powers justify their legitimacy? Weber thus proposes his theory of three pure forms of possible legitimation: tradition, charisma, and legal rationality.[5]

---

4. Max Weber, "Politics as a Vocation," in *Max Weber: Essays in Sociology*, ed. and trans. H. H. Gerth and C. Wright Mills (New York: Oxford University Press, 1946), 77.
5. Ibid., 79.

Of course, considering reasons for submission is an invaluable exercise. But it's nonetheless shocking that similar questions aren't raised about violence. Here, we have a theory about ways in which the state can legitimize itself; so why do we not have a theory about forms of violence? States are distinguished from one another according to the justifications on which they are based; couldn't the same be done according to the kind of violence they exercise or use? Why does violence seem to be regarded as a secondary concern in relation to legitimacy?

The idea of "legitimate violence" is what prompts a change in focus. The issue of the legitimization of violence takes center stage, to the detriment of the problem of violence. The field of analysis has concentrated on modes of legitimization—for instance, on the way in which states come to be recognized when they exercise their functions. The question of domination has become one of forms of legitimacy and legitimization. And violence is no longer constructed as an object of analysis in its own right but has become absent from sociological reasoning. What kinds of violence does the law exert? How? Against whom? By what means? These questions are ignored, as if violence was a nonobject, a form of inherently transparent action, which can't be dissected or described. As a matter of fact, it's only when the state acts in defiance of the norms on which it's based and which legitimize it—police misconduct, inequalities in judicial processing, arbitrary exercises of power—that it is designated as "violent."

DISMANTLING LEGITIMACY

I'm not suggesting that the formulation of a lucid theory about the state requires the rejection of Weber's argument. But neither do I think it sufficient to simply supplement studies of legitimacy with research on official violence. Rather, I wonder if it wouldn't be better to change the way we use the idea of "legitimate violence" and from there develop a completely different approach to this characterization of the state. If it's true that the state successfully claims a monopoly of legitimate physical violence, then shouldn't critical thought position itself laterally with respect to the stakes of legitimacy? Its task would then be to find instruments that identify, reveal, and demonstrate violence in places where we no longer see it. *If violence is perceived as legitimate, if it is accepted, taken for granted, and therefore viewed as something that can't be transformed or criticized, then the intellectual's role is less to understand the reasons for that perception than to deconstruct it.* We must take a step back from the problematic of recognition in order to reveal the state as it truly is and therefore allow individuals—meaning every one of us—to become aware of and viscerally experience the true violence exercised by the state.

It's not by chance that both political philosophy and the social sciences impede the revelation and awareness of state violence. Political theory, originating with Kant, and political science, with Weber, share the same fundamental bias, which dooms them to act as epistemological obstacles: they view the state as a distinct entity, incommensurable with other entities that make up the social world. They examine the state differently than they would any other entity: studying its foundations in the case of Kantians, studying its modes of legitimization in the case of Weberians. These approaches share the same goal: to characterize the *state's specificity*. For that matter, the fact that these two investigative models take the form of distinct and relatively autonomous disciplines or specialties within academia—political philosophy and political science—indicates widespread acceptance of the notion that the state represents a specific object, and not an object like any other that should be approached through shared methods and questions.

But by granting the state such specificity, by approaching it with specific tools and conceptualizing it in a specific way (in terms of legitimacy, foundations, etc.), we effectively become its prisoner; we give the state what it wants at the very moment we claim to be viewing it objectively. These are perspectives embedded within the state apparatus itself; they take for granted the state's claims and assertions even while positing it as their object of study. Political theory and political science ratify the division that the state strives to make between itself and other actors in order to affirm its official authority. Indeed, rather than questioning, analyzing, or revealing that division, these two models take it as their point of departure. In the end, by granting the state the exceptional status from which it draws its authority, they do not so much take sovereignty as an object of study as they do participate in its functioning and constitution. Owing to their very mode of inquiry, these endeavors are less a matter of investigating the state than of symbolic statism. They treat the state with deference, respect, and attention, thus granting it, in the realm of language, the submission it demands. Political science and political philosophy form submissive and obliging positivities.

When Pierre Bourdieu reproached Weber for having focused, in his definition, on the *physical* violence of the state and having overlooked its *symbolic* violence, he meant precisely to draw attention to the fact that one of the state's essential characteristics is to influence representations, transform perceptions, and shape our ways of seeing in an infraconscious manner.

The logic of the state consists of masking its actions and passing them off as something else. *The state is the authority that successfully passes off its violent actions as nonviolent.* Consequently, a critical theory of the state requires that a mechanism be invented that allows us to conceptualize the state without adopting its logic, or, as Bourdieu puts it, without "applying categories of thought [and perception, we might add] produced by the state."[6] We must reveal not only the state's physical violence but also its symbolic violence, which allows it to impose its constraints without them being perceived as such by its victims—the subjects of the law. Just because a violent action is not perceived as such, or because it is legitimate, or because we consent to it, does not mean it disappears or is any less violent. On the contrary, it remains violent, but it is unrecognized as such. The scholar's task is to dismantle that ignorance or misunderstanding in order to describe things *as they truly are*.

EXCEPTION

We know that there is a link between sovereignty and exceptionalism—that is, that the sovereign has the right to impose a state of emergency and suspend the law in the name of the protection and self-preservation of the political and social body. Sovereign power is defined by its singular capacity to emancipate itself from the law thanks to a special status that allows it to define what an exception is and to then invoke said exception in order to suspend the regular rule of law and therefore give itself (and only itself) the possibility of no longer having to follow it.[7]

Of course, suspension of the law occurs—but rarely and temporarily. This possibility defines the structure and shape of sovereignty, though in reality, it remains, by definition, rare—in other words, exceptional.

Nonetheless, when it comes to language, this "exceptional" status appears to be permanent and structural. The state has the

---

6. Pierre Bourdieu, "Esprits d'État," in *Raisons pratiques* (Paris: Seuil, 1994), 101.
7. Jacques Derrida, *The Death Penalty: Volume I*, ed. Geoffrey Bennington, Marc Crépon, and Thomas Dutoit, trans. Peggy Kamuf (Chicago: University of Chicago Press, 2014), 85–87; Giorgio Agamben, *State of Exception*, trans. Kevin Attell (Chicago: University of Chicago Press, 2005).

capacity to ensure that we speak differently of it than we do of private actions, problematize it in a specific way, and use specific words and terms to designate what it does. This way of excepting the state, of treating it differently, is proof of the unconscious and spontaneous recognition we accord it. Here, the political issue is linked directly to the linguistic one in that reserving a vocabulary specific to the state equates to validating its claim to incarnate a superior, transcendent, and unassailable authority. We are thus inclined to accept its claim to legitimacy and its exceptional nature, meaning we view it using categories created by the state itself.

In his seminar on the death penalty, Jacques Derrida adheres to that system when underlining that, in his opinion, we can't understand the logic of the death penalty unless we reject a certain abolitionist discourse that insists on the sacred nature of life. We tend, maintains Derrida, to oppose the death penalty in the name of "respect for life" and the "right to life." If the state forbids murder, and considers it to be the ultimate transgression, how can it then claim the right to kill?

According to Derrida, this argument is overly facile. Most of all, it is unconvincing. (Note that Derrida is clearly not arguing in favor of the death penalty: on the contrary, he explores what it means to maintain an abolitionist discourse.) That is because, insists Derrida, criticizing the state because it carries out actions forbidden to individuals reflects a misunderstanding of political logic. The very conception of the state supposes its exceptional character. It can detain people, whereas individuals can't; it can force people to surrender a part of their property (through taxes), whereas individuals can't (that would be theft). Consequently, the interdiction to murder in no way contradicts the existence of the death penalty; if it did, the ban on illegal confinement could just as easily be used as an argument against imprisonment.

According to Derrida, critical discourse about the death penalty can only become solid and consequential if it is transformed. It must acknowledge the fact that the death penalty doesn't oppose life and that therefore it is pointless to challenge it with the "right to life" argument. In reality the death penalty stands in opposition to murder in the same way that prison does to arbitrary detention. The law can therefore state simultaneously, and without contradiction, "thou shalt not kill" and "if you commit such an act, I will kill you," because it's neither the same death nor the same action.[8] There are therefore two different and incommensurable ways to take a life: the first—murder—is arbitrary and anarchical; the second—the death penalty—is regulated, organized, and legal. There is "no relation of affinity, in this logic, between murder and the death penalty, between murder outside the law and the legal death penalty."[9] Abolitionist discourse must confront that difference and grasp the death penalty in its singularity if it wants to avoid formulaic rhetoric and be both effective and credible.

The complexity of the abolitionist discourse and the cleverness of arguments in favor of the death penalty highlighted by Derrida are undeniably important and should be taken into account. But I find myself wondering whether it's possible, and even necessary, to say precisely the opposite of what Derrida says. We can question the pertinence of the idea that it's essential to acknowledge a difference between state actions and private actions, thus ensuring that critical logic cannot employ the same rhetoric to designate actions occurring in these two spheres. This is because that approach assumes recognition of the state, the law, and any divisions they decree at the very moment when we should, in fact, be trying to understand these institutions' operations and violence. This mode of

---

8. Derrida, *The Death Penalty*, 1:9–14.
9. Ibid., 14.

analysis presupposes sovereignty, the sovereign exception, and the state's right to undertake actions forbidden to us. It is a paradigm that applies sovereign-created categories to the sovereign power itself and may consequently legitimize the actions of this power. In this case language masks reality by behaving as if the state acts differently than it really does.

But isn't it precisely by refusing the state's exceptional nature, by questioning the logic according to which state actions are of a different nature than individual ones, that we can truly construct a critical discourse of the criminal justice system and the state in general? Simply put, this approach would entail stating the truth—what the state actually does. From there we would truly be able to examine what is permissible or necessary and what isn't. In other words, the approach suggested here isn't intended to destroy or reject the state, or to invalidate its existence and actions, but rather to find ways to avoid basing our thinking on mystifications and to elucidate what the state is and does in order to evaluate what is not acceptable and, on the contrary, what is.

SIMPLIFY AND NAME

It's vital to challenge the way of thinking about the state that we find in political philosophy (Arendt and Habermas), political science (Weber), and, more recently, the Derrida seminar cited above with another approach that breaks with the political use of language and treats the state like any other actor, thereby demystifying it.

One of the rare writers to have proposed an understanding of the state free of error or ignorance and who can therefore serve as our guide and model, was Friedrich Nietzsche in his analyses of the logic of remorse and the guilty conscience. In *On the Genealogy of Morality* Nietzsche effectively challenges the idea that punishment can provoke remorse deep down in a criminal's soul. Justice wants to produce remorse. It is intended to reform the delinquent by sowing a guilty conscience, encouraging him to reform himself and to normalize his behavior. The "popular conscience" also desires punishment, which it views as an instrument destined to arouse a "sense of guilt" within the transgressor. In other words, one of the most common justifications for punishment is its "moral utility." But according to Nietzsche, that view is false; historically, it has been proven wrong. Criminal procedures and punishments do not produce remorse:

> Punishment is alleged to have the value of awakening the *feeling of guilt* in the guilty party, in it is sought the actual *instrumentum* of the psychical reaction called "bad conscience," and "sting of conscience." But in doing so we desecrate reality and psychology even for today: and how much more so for the longest period of human history, its prehistory! *The genuine sting of conscience is something extremely rare precisely among criminals and prisoners*; the prisons and jails are *not* breeding grounds where this species of gnawing worm prefers to thrive:—on this all conscientious observers agree, who in many cases abandon such a judgment reluctantly enough and against their deepest inclinations.[10]

So Nietzsche asks: Why doesn't justice provoke remorse? Why doesn't punishment cause regret and a guilty conscience? Why is there an antithetical relationship between the logic of punishment and the logic of remorse? For, on reflection, it appears evident that the act of punishment can ultimately only provoke the opposite of a guilty conscience. Indeed, its sole effect may be to harden criminals. The belief that punishment will lead criminals to improve themselves and renounce violence is a delusion: it overlooks the

---

10. Friedrich Nietzsche, *On the Genealogy of Morality*, in *Beyond Good and Evil / On the Genealogy of Morality*, trans. Adrian Del Caro, vol. 8 of *The Complete Works of Friedrich Nietzsche* (Stanford, CA: Stanford University Press, 2014), 269–70 (second emphasis added).

violence of criminal procedures and punishments, which ensures that the state isn't a virtuous example to be imitated. Why not? Because the state treats criminals in the same way that criminals themselves would—implying that their actions are not in themselves reprehensible, that in fact there is nothing about which the criminal should feel guilty. The state responds to crimes with actions that are not only comparable but also similar and identical to them in every way. As a result, criminals are unable to understand why and for what they should reproach themselves:

> But if we think instead of those millennia *before* human history, then we can judge unhesitatingly that precisely through punishment the development of the feeling of guilt has been most strongly *hindered*—at least with respect to the victims on whom the punishing force vented itself. For we should not underestimate the extent to which *the criminal himself is hindered by the very sight of judicial and executive procedures from perceiving his deed*, the nature of his deed, as reprehensible *in itself*: after all, he sees the exact same kind of deeds practiced in the service of justice and then approved, and practiced with good conscience: thus spying, deception, bribery, setting traps, the whole sneaky and underhanded art of the police and prosecutors, then the robbing, overpowering, slandering, taking prisoner, torturing, murdering as they unfold in the different kinds of punishment, on principle and lacking even the excuse of emotion—all of them by no means actions *in themselves* repudiated and condemned by his judges, but only in a certain respect and practical application. "Bad conscience," this most uncanny and interesting plant of our earthly vegetation, did *not* grow from this soil.[11]

---

11. Ibid., 270 (some emphases added).

This Nietzsche text provides an exact counterpoint to Derrida's argument. It relies on a symbolic coup d'état and a reappropriation of language and of our nominative ability that is based on rejecting perceptions the state attempts to impose. By adopting Nietzsche's approach, we can see that, contrary to Derrida, and therefore to the theses of Weber and Arendt, it is impossible to understand the state's actions unless we reject its own efforts to conceal them, which entails our acceptance of the idea of an equivalence or, better still, a similarity between state actions and private actions. Rather than saying that the state "sentences to death," we must say that it kills; that it doesn't arrest individuals but "abducts" them; that it doesn't imprison people but "wrongfully detains" them; that it doesn't force them to pay fines but "robs" them.

A notable example comes from an excerpt from the Fourteenth Amendment to the United States Constitution: "No state shall make or enforce any law which shall abridge the privileges or immunities of citizens of the United States; nor shall any state deprive any person of life, liberty, or property, without due process of law." This text is somewhat of a lie, which conceals and glosses over reality. It isn't enough to say that the state "deprives" us of life, liberty, or property: it kills us, confines us, and steals from us. The fact that it does so in accordance with the law, legally, in no way diminishes the reality of what is occurring and the violence of the actions taken. Viewing the state objectively thus requires a translation. Telling the truth would entail revising the amendment as follows: "No state shall kill, confine, or steal without due process of law." Only such wording would express the reality of the repressive state apparatus (for that matter, any study of punishment, sentencing, and policing that does not begin with a transparent vision of the state will be condemned to founding itself on mystification and unable to present itself as rational).

And incidentally, doesn't the state say as much? At times, in its laws, the state doesn't appear to be hiding its actions. Once again, everything seems to indicate that we wear blinders and lie to ourselves. After all, the state affirms its practical commensurability with other social actors. Take, for example, the text of article 224-1 of the French penal code on abduction and illegal restraint: "The arrest, abduction, detention or imprisonment of a person *without an order from an established authority and outside the cases provided by law* is punished by twenty years' criminal imprisonment."[12] In other words, the act being explicitly punished is not the abduction, detention, or imprisonment of a person but the act of doing so without the state's permission. Put another way, not only does the state abduct individuals; it *says* that it does.

Seeing and sensing the state as it truly is requires, paradoxically, that we dissolve it as an object. A lucid perspective necessitates that we restore the state's banality by treating it as something other than itself. This leads to the thought that perhaps Elias's approach to the state is superior to Weber's. Elias essentially compares the state to a protection racket: "A protection racket organized by gangsters, such as you have in Chicago, is not so very different from the state."[13] I understand the objection of Bourdieu, who reproaches this definition for its reductionism and for not noting that the state is not exactly *perceived* as a protection racket.[14] But to be fair, successfully sensing and revealing state violence by challenging actors' established perceptions should be both the objective and outcome of any critical sociological analysis. Real thinking can be defined as the refusal to believe that an initial and popular perception of

---

12. Translation source: www.legifrance.gouv.fr (emphasis added).
13. Quoted in Pierre Bourdieu, *On the State: Lectures at the Collège de France, 1989–1992*, ed. Patrick Champagne, Rémi Lenoir, Franck Poupeau, and Marie-Christine Rivière (Cambridge: Polity, 2014), 129; see also Norbert Elias, *The Civilizing Process* (Oxford: Blackwell, 2000).
14. Bourdieu, *On the State*.

the world is necessarily true.[15] The theorist's role is not to recreate actors' spontaneous experiences of the world or to understand the reasons behind them; doing so would merely strengthen established perceptions. On the contrary, the theorist should inflict violence on actors, disrupt them, and find ways to challenge their frameworks and visions of the world. If actors recognize themselves in a given analysis, that analysis only consolidates and preserves what has already been established. And this is a problem.

Reducing the state to what it is, naming things as they really are, and borrowing a common language to conceptualize the state allows us to avoid political mystifications and deconstruct entrenched notions. Here, criticism implies criticism of the state, or criticism of the state's claim to be what it is. Any analysis of violence and the law must refuse the autonomy claimed by politics; it must employ a nonpolitical vocabulary to contextualize and understand politics. If we hope to challenge existing modes of governance, we can't continue to be governed by the language and categories produced by the state.

This is why I suggested, in my book *Michel Foucault's Last Lesson*, that it is possible to find a critical dimension at work in the neoliberal paradigm and in the way in which its theorists use economic reasoning to think about the state. Economics applies the same categories to the state that it uses for all social actors; it accords them no special treatment. It understands the state through the same concepts of markets, supply and demand, cost/benefit calculations, and utility. Neoliberalism refuses to recognize the state as special or exceptional, viewing it as one reality among many, commensurable to others. It applies an analytical framework to the state that functions for all other institutions. The economic

---

15. See Joan W. Scott, "The Evidence of Experience," in *Critical Theory* 17, no. 4 (1991): 773–79.

perspective dissolves the exceptional character of the state and allows us to consider it in a demythologized form.

This method has a wider applicability: regardless of its subject, the construction of an analysis that reveals the true functioning of the social world requires a break with the self-fabricated images of activities and the self-established representations of actors. The social world is built of preconstructed facts, and this is how we perceive it. Critical thought shouldn't strengthen that preconstruction but, on the contrary, deconstruct it and consider ways in which to reveal its deceptive form.[16]

Incidentally, this is one of the main lessons we can take away from the attitude informing the approach of Bourdieu. Throughout his work—and, paradoxically, he was reproached for this—Bourdieu used the vocabulary of economics to address the different activities that make up the social world: he questioned religion, language, culture, and even literature in terms of markets, capital, supply and demand, interest, competition, revenue, and profit. Thinking of things in this way strips them of any unique or special status they may claim or foreground; it repositions them in a general framework and therefore has a simultaneously revelatory and disenchanting effect that allows us to see them in a new light. Reductionism becomes the point of departure for a lucid analysis of the social world.

To return to the main subject of this chapter: I am, of course, aware that using plain language to refer to the state ("theft," "abduct," "kill," "confine") can shock and upset. We're not used to seeing these terms in this context. And such designations may appear to betray an inordinately antistatist impulse. This is not the case. But we would likely do better to invert the problem and to ask

---

16. See Didier Eribon, *La Société comme verdict* (Paris: Fayard, 2013).

what mechanisms of dissimulation and obstruction are at work that prevent us from feeling the violence of the state in all of its reality.

The scholarly approach aims to give us the means to become aware of the powers to which we are unconsciously exposed. It should enable us to clearly evaluate how tolerable a situation is or—on the contrary—how intolerable and, therefore, how much it must be transformed. To be sure, saying what the state is and showing what it truly does fosters and gives new life to a resistant attitude. But it also, and above all, claims our right to a certain intransigence. Given the sway that the legal-political order holds over our lives, it's *normal* to go as far as possible when taking a hard look at its operations. It is on this condition that we equip ourselves with the requisite tools for reflecting on the reality of the state and thereby establishing the rational foundations on which to base both the demands that we can rightfully make of it and the powers that we may or may not be ready to accord it.

PART THREE
THE SYSTEM OF JUDGMENT

BEYOND RESPONSIBILITY

It suffices to attend a few trials in succession to quickly realize that they all unfold in the same way. Each court proceeding follows a well-established logic. And even though a reform of French criminal procedure was introduced during the writing of this book, the general trial structure has remained entirely unchanged. Everything takes place in a completely monotonous way. Presiding judges and prosecutors change, of course, as do defendants and their lawyers. Alleged crimes and their circumstances differ, and witnesses come from varied milieus and tell very specific stories. But this variability in criminal matters doesn't affect the structure of the system of judgment itself. Though trials closely resemble one another, that uniformity can't be attributed to the criminal code, which is ultimately rather vague when it comes to how court proceedings are held.

In France trials unfold as follows. The presiding judge asks the defendant to state his or her identity: first and last name, age, profession, and place of residence. Next the court proceeds with random jury selection. Then the actual trial begins: the presiding judge summarizes the charges against the defendant and the reasons he or she has been summoned.

Next comes that strange moment when the court takes an interest in the defendant's life and personality. The accused is questioned at length, sometimes for several hours, on personal tastes, habits, and character, before the facts have even been debated by each side and the question of guilt examined. The presiding judges of criminal trial courts, though rarely very intelligent individuals, are nonetheless quite proud of making what they believe to be discerning statements (a belief seconded by others in an effort to win these judges' goodwill). They justify this sequence of events, during which anything and everything is discussed except for the "crime" itself, or the defendant's potential involvement, by the idea that "to judge is to understand." The court therefore endeavors to "understand" the trajectory of the "accused." Often, a specialized investigator (a "personality detective") recounts the defendant's *curriculum vitae* and divulges details about his or her life.

Then comes a string of witnesses and experts who talk about the facts or shed light on the circumstances in question: police officers or gendarmes who led the investigation, medical examiners, psychiatrists, individuals who witnessed the accused acts, etc. Between testimonies, the presiding judge may show photos of the crime scene or read depositions from individuals who were not called as witnesses. On one or two occasions (rarely more as the defendant says very little during the trial), the presiding judge will ask the person being charged to react to what's been said, explain his or her role (or lack thereof) in the alleged crime, and to elaborate on any contradictions.

Finally, it's time for arguments and petitions. Plaintiffs, if they exist, speak first, followed by the prosecutor, and then the defense attorneys. The defendant is then granted a moment to speak one final time if he or she so desires. Finally, the court and jurors withdraw to deliberate—and then comes the verdict.

Admittedly, despite the boredom of attending a trial, one quickly gets caught up in the game. I don't see how it's possible to resist it, nor who could resist it, but one does find oneself rapidly adopting a subjective position similar to that of the judge: one wonders about the defendant's guilt, his or her degree of responsibility or involvement, whether his or her actions were premeditated or not, the veracity of his or her statements in regard to what was said by witnesses or experts, and their trustworthiness. At the end of the trial, when the presiding judge reads the questions he will have to answer during deliberations with the other judges and the jurors to determine whether the defendant is guilty—"Is X guilty of deliberately killing Y?" or "Were his actions premeditated?" or "Is X guilty of deliberately destroying property? Was the act committed by an organized group? In connection with a terrorist organization?" or "Is the defendant guilty of committing an act of sexual penetration against Y?" "Was the act committed at gunpoint?" and so forth—no one is surprised. It seems logical to formulate the questions in this way. They correspond to reality. And the answers come to mind naturally as well. Thus, not only are the questions asked unproblematic but, in almost all cases, neither are the answers. In other words, it's hard to see how it would be possible to answer with anything other than "yes" if you were in the jurors' place.

This demonstration of the self-evident nature of the judicial process shows that the trial constitutes a logical apparatus, that it's not only coherent but is also endowed with an inescapable internal logic. Once we enter this arena, it's already late in the game. What is on display is part of a broader structure whose impacts occur unbeknownst to us and in which everything therefore unfolds seamlessly.

Frameworks organize the judicial world and our relationship to it. But these frameworks are no longer visible during a trial. They predetermine the logic of the criminal system. They mold our experience. Paradoxically, understanding what happens during a trial requires not that we enter a courtroom to note what we see there, but that we leave it. We have to break away from our spontaneous perceptions of the court in order to effect a critical reconstitution of ourselves—and thereby grasp the ways of constructing and relating to the world that make penal logic, and our adhesion to it, possible. We must step back from ourselves if we want to understand the categories, ideologies, and narratives that undergird the logic of the criminal system and the judicial mechanism and give shape to what we call "justice."

RESPONSIBILITY

All theory has a history. Every intellectual approach is created and defined based on preexisting and transmitted questions, concepts, premises, and perspectives. Even thoughts or opinions that claim to be the most critical or the most innovative are born of tradition; they manipulate entrenched notions and often even demonstrate their radicalism by taking up approaches that indicate their kinship with a given sector of theory.

Any intellectual reflection is formed, often unconsciously, according to the modes and forms that precede and guide it. In this way, when I set out to analyze the logic behind the system of judgment, to understand how the state affects and treats us, the category that struck me as an obvious starting point, as if made available for deconstruction by traditional criticism, was that of responsibility. Legal theory and legal criticism share the following diagnosis: the order of law is based on the establishment of a responsible subject. Being a subject of the law means being treated as an entity to whom a certain number of behaviors are imputed and who must eventually, if those behaviors break a law, answer for them. The law is therefore synonymous with the establishment of an apparatus that organizes a system of sanctions and punishments and that attributes behaviors to entities so that they can suffer the consequences.[1]

Accentuating responsibility means insisting on the fact that punitive criminal proceedings are less about linking us to the law than linking us to ourselves so that we can be treated as the "authors" of what we do and have done and thus be subjected to punishment. The idea of responsibility alone appears to pave the way for the establishment of a system of judgment. Similarly, the critical immunity enjoyed by that system seems to stem, first and foremost, from our adhesion to the idea of the responsible subject. Indeed, it's difficult to question the idea of judgment when we think in terms of responsibility: from the moment we accept the subject as a being responsible for his actions, how can we imagine that he shouldn't answer for them and assume the consequences? The existence of individual responsibility for one's actions legitimizes the act of judging. It further allows for the legitimization of the criminal justice system as an instrument not only to punish but also to dissuade: the individual is presumed to be the conscious, intentional, and voluntary author of his acts, such that the possibility of punishment is likely to spur him to renounce criminal action.

It's therefore not by chance that legal criticisms that target the very heart of the criminal justice system have focused on the operation through which the law connects who we are to what we've done (to our past) and forces us to address it. The law establishes identities, stabilizes the self, and obliges us to coincide with a past, instead of offering the means to free ourselves from it. Consequently, legal critique has often consisted of opposing the idea of the person, of a coherent substance, with that of an incoher-

---

1. See H. L. A. Hart, *Punishment and Responsibility: Essays in the Philosophy of Law* (Oxford: Oxford University Press, 2008).

ent, scattered, splintered being—that is, of opposing the memory of the past to the right to forget. Nietzsche was one of the first to introduce this approach in *On the Genealogy of Morality*: the law is embedded in a process whereby people are domesticated; they are made to coincide with themselves and are endowed with a will that obligates them across time; that makes them responsible. The law originates in the economic logic of debt and of promises: one's word is one's bond. The individual as subject of the law is formed by the connection between the present self and the past self and the fact that the former must answer for actions taken by the latter; the two are connected by an intangible that we call the "responsible self" and who can make promises independently.[2] This analysis is one of the essential elements of Walter Benjamin's *Critique of Violence*, according to which the law's foundational violence comes from the act of creating a responsible subject in situations where revolutionary action would consist of undoing the operation that subjugates us to the order of responsibility.

I am not, of course, denying the importance of thinking about the question of responsibility. Clearly, one of the kinds of violence the law inflicts on us is the way in which it binds us to what we've already done without allowing us the space to forget or the possibility to escape, reinvent ourselves, or flee.

Nevertheless, I believe that insisting on this notion may cause us to overlook what is truly essential. This picture is insufficient and doesn't allow us to go far enough in our understanding of what is at stake within the order of law—and of what happens during a trial. I'd like to challenge the idea according to which the notion of responsibility represents the pivotal point around which our judi-

---

2. Friedrich Nietzsche, *On the Genealogy of Morality*, in *Beyond Good and Evil / On the Genealogy of Morality*, trans. Adrian Del Caro, vol. 8 of *The Complete Works of Friedrich Nietzsche* (Stanford, CA: Stanford University Press, 2014), 252–53.

cial system rotates and, by extension, the relevance of theories that place this notion at the heart of any reflection on the law.

THE RIGHT OF IRRESPONSIBILITY

For anyone who understands criminal law, it's logical to deconstruct the link between penality and responsibility. Every modern criminal system, for example in Europe or the United States, offers conditions under which a subject can be held responsible for his or her actions and/or can be punished.[3] Every criminal system also anticipates cases in which an individual cannot be held criminally responsible for what he or she has done or cannot be punished: those conditions may have to do with the subject himself (for example, his mental condition) or the circumstances of his actions (for example, in the case of self-defense). Depending on the system, these cases may result in a situation whereby a subject who has indeed committed an illegal act is not held criminally responsible, is not judged, or is found guilty but not sentenced.

Let's examine, for example, the French criminal code. After a few general provisions, the criminal code immediately and at length addresses the definition of "criminal responsibility." This notion appears to support the entire edifice that follows. While it is true that this section aims to define what being "criminally responsible" means, it's important to keep in mind that it simultaneously endeavors to reflect on and declare the lack of responsibility, or irresponsibility, of certain subjects. In other words, the justice system doesn't only recognize responsible individuals. The law doesn't only create responsible subjects. It also organizes the irresponsibility of certain actors under certain circumstances. *The French criminal code chapter on responsibility defines both the conditions of responsibility and irresponsibility.*

---

3. H. L. A. Hart, "Legal Responsibility and Excuses," in *Punishment and Responsibility*, 28, 188–90.

After stating that "no one is criminally responsible except for his own conduct," the criminal code stipulates, "there is no felony or misdemeanor in the absence of an intent to commit it." It then outlines the "grounds for absence or attenuation of liability," establishing a list that indicates how the law can *also* create irresponsibility:

- A person is not criminally responsible who, when the act was committed, was suffering from a psychological or neuropsychological disorder which destroyed his discernment or his ability to control his actions.
- A person is not criminally responsible who acted under the influence of a force or constraint which he could not resist.
- A person is not criminally responsible who establishes that he believed he could legitimately perform the action because of a mistake of law that he was not in a position to avoid.
- A person is not criminally responsible who performs an act prescribed or authorized by legislative or regulatory provisions.
- A person is not criminally responsible who performs an action commanded by a lawful authority, unless the action is manifestly unlawful.
- A person is not criminally responsible if, confronted with an unjustified attack upon himself or upon another, he performs at that moment an action compelled by the necessity of self-defense or the defense of another person, except where the means of defense used are not proportionate to the seriousness of the attack.
- A person is not criminally responsible if, to interrupt the commission of a felony or a misdemeanor against property, he performs an act of defense other than willful murder, where the act is strictly necessary for the intended objective [and if] the means used are proportionate to the gravity of the offence.

- A person is not criminally responsible if confronted with a present or imminent danger to himself, another person or property, he performs an act necessary to ensure the safety of the person or property, except where the means used are disproportionate to the seriousness of the threat.[4]

This list is moving and quite important, and I find it worth including in its entirety. It reveals an essential dimension of the state that any analysis of the workings of the law must take into account and that has too often been ignored or underemphasized: the state's ability not to judge, or not to convict, meaning not to hold individuals responsible for their actions. In other words, it's not correct to say that the state binds us to ourselves because, in fact, it also offers the possibility of disassociating ourselves from what we've done. The law creates both responsible and irresponsible subjects. Undeniably, the idea of responsibility plays an essential role in the legal order, but it isn't sufficient for understanding its actions.

That is why we can envisage radically reversing normal perceptions and grasping the workings of the law in a manner different from classic theory. After all, if we had to single out the specific character of the law and the state, what would it be? Wouldn't it be that, in comparison with systems of vengeance, vendettas, and spontaneous reactions to trauma that drive us to inflict punishment, those systems introduce protections and immunities? Can we not legitimately consider that the specificity of the law in fact resides not in the creation of responsible subjects but, on the con-

---

4. From Article 122 of the Criminal Code of the French Republic (as of 2005), with the participation of John Rason Spencer, QC, Professor of Law, University of Cambridge, Fellow of Selwyn College. A PDF of the English translation is available at www.legislationline.org/documents/section/criminal-codes/country/30 (translation slightly modified). The translation speaks of being "liable," where I have preferred to use the word *responsible*.

trary, *in the creation of irresponsible subjects—in the creation of a category of irresponsibility*? In a sense, if we had to identify the essence of the modern justice system, what best characterizes it, we would paradoxically have to search among those instances when, for whatever reason, owing to this or that rational requirement, it decides not to judge or not to punish someone.

The theorist H. L. A. Hart even claims that ultimately irresponsibility can be considered the primary category of modern law. On close study of legal provisions and precedents, he notes, one will find that the law never provides a clear and precise definition of what being "criminally responsible" means. It never spells out the conditions—in terms of will and intent—that must be met for a subject to be found responsible. In other words, responsibility isn't defined positively but negatively. It's only once an individual has broken the law without being able to cite a basis for irresponsibility that he or she is assumed responsible.[5] Thus, Hart concludes that in the end one could almost say that the law assumes we are not responsible and that it is only when conditions eliminating responsibility are not met that we are deemed "responsible": the absence of irresponsibility determines responsibility.

ACTION

Understanding the workings of the law and the underpinnings of the justice system requires that we look beyond the idea of responsibility. It's not accurate to say that the law positions us as responsible subjects. It can also determine our irresponsibility and dissociate us from what we've done. We therefore have to shift our perspective and reconsider what it means to be a subject of the law.

Fundamentally, theories about the law and the state that cen-

---

5. H. L. A. Hart, "Legal Responsibility and Excuses," 28.

ter on responsibility attempt to identify what the law produces in terms of subjects. They concentrate on the figure of the individual created by the legal-political system. I'd like to suggest another point of view: the law does not first and foremost deploy a "philosophy of the subject" (it creates both responsible and irresponsible subjects). Before relying on the idea that the subject is a being responsible for and conscious of his or her actions, on a philosophy of action and intent, the criminal justice system relies on a construction of reality and a way of perceiving the world. The criminal justice system operates in accordance with a view to which we already adhere—namely, that acts, whatever happens to each of us, are attributable to an author. Justice places us within a perceptual universe or, rather, is itself embedded within a broader system of perceptions, within which assigning responsibility for damages, injuries, and aggressions to an individual (or to several individuals treated separately) appears self-evident. The reason or cause for what happens in the world—what happens to me—must be sought in an individual and his or her actions.

The question of responsibility, within the state apparatus, is secondary. It is only posed after the fact. The system of judgment first deploys an individualizing construction of events. It imputes actions to individuals. Only then can it begin to identify the eventual criminal responsibility of the subject behind the "criminal act" and from there determine the punishment he or she merits, if one is merited.

What's more, the secondary nature of the question of responsibility appears in the French criminal code itself, specifically when it addresses the situation in which "one of the grounds for criminal irresponsibility . . . is cited as part of the case for the defense"—put another way, when the defense argues the defendant's irresponsibility, during a trial, and asks that the defendant not be convicted. In this case, notes the French code (article 349-1), the court and jurors must answer the two following questions during their deliberations:

1. Did the accused commit this act?
2. Does the accused benefit in respect of this act from the ground of criminal irresponsibility provided for in article . . . of the Criminal Code, according to which a person is not criminally responsible who . . . ? [sic][6]

A trial can very easily proceed even when the defendant is "irresponsible"—or, rather, he will be declared irresponsible by the court and jurors. As a result, the logic of the court operates outside the question of responsibility. Its initial aim is to link events that occur in the world to individuals. The system of judgment simultaneously constructs and presupposes an individualizing narration of what happens. Events or acts in society can be attributed to a single author who, eventually, will have to answer for what she did, if she is seen as responsible for her actions.

We often use the category of "individual responsibility" when seeking to identify the fundamental principles of our criminal justice system: everyone is individually responsible for his or her own actions, or, as the criminal code states, "no one is criminally liable except for his own conduct." But contrary to what we may believe, it's not the word *responsibility* in the expression "individual responsibility" that is most important but rather the adjective *individual*. In other words, the foundation of the repressive apparatus, and what makes the idea of punishment and repressive actions possible, is not a specific figure of the subject (who is presented as free and

---

6. From Article 349-1 of the Criminal Procedure Code of the French Republic (as of 2006), with the participation of John Rason Spencer, QC, Professor of Law, University of Cambridge, Fellow of Selwyn College. A PDF of the English translation is available at www.legislationline.org/documents/section/criminal-codes/country/30 (translation slightly modified).

responsible for his or her actions) but a perception of what is happening: the system of judgment assumes that we see the world in a certain way and that we understand what goes on in a specific way. The criminal justice system creates and relies on an individualizing narrative; when something happens, the cause must be sought out in an individual's action. Once this perception is established, the possibility of judgment emerges.

It now becomes clearer why so much time is spent, during a trial, discussing a defendant's life, character, friends, history, and relationships. Several functions are served by that biographical focus (a point to which I will return), meaning the persistent tendency within criminal justice to concentrate on biographical details that teach us nothing about the facts. But one of them is to create the system of judgment and punishment. The interest in a defendant's biographical details sets the stage that allows the criminal system to operate: the act on one side, the individual on the other. Thereafter, the trial will hinge on deciding whether the two can be linked.

Is it possible to consider those acts in a nonindividualizing framework? What would happen if we dismantled this perceptual framework and constructed other narratives? If we understood the logics behind events and actions differently? What other conception of judgment and law might emerge? What other perception of justice and what is "just" and "fair" might be imagined?

THE POLITICS
OF PERCEPTIONS

I'm well aware that the system of individual responsibility, or, more precisely, of the individualization of perceptions, appears self-evident. It organizes our spontaneous understanding of reality. For that matter, it is difficult to know whether the state constructs and imposes this system or merely appropriates and deploys it. Either way, the fact remains that linking an act to an author, and questioning whether the latter can be held responsible for the former, seems to be an operation that merely reflects an undeniable reality.

That notion is imposed on us with such force and such a sense of inevitability that even an author like Hans Kelsen treats it as a nonissue, a prejuridical and preontological given: a fact. This is extremely significant given that Kelsen, in *Pure Theory of Law*, otherwise claims to completely break with realism and maintain the autonomy of the legal sphere in relation to empirical or natural considerations—hence the idea to establish a pure theory of law, meaning an autonomous legal theory, without reference to elements exterior to the legal sphere or ones that can't at any rate acquire meaning within that sphere unless the law qualifies them as juridical facts. Yet the "purity" of his theory is based on an impurity and appears contaminated by naive empiricism.

Kelsen dedicates a paragraph of this major work to the opposition between "collective responsibility" and "individual responsibility." Note that the focus here isn't the idea of responsibility, since it exists in both systems being analyzed, but the transition from a collective conception of behaviors and events to an individual one. Kelsen examines legal systems to determine to what or whom the idea of responsibility is applied: a collective or an individual, the delinquent.

Individual responsibility designates a system in which a sanction, if one is necessary, targets an individual: the delinquent is presented as the author of the prohibited act. With collective responsibility the sanction is not directed against an individual but against a group to which the delinquent usually, though not necessarily, belongs. Kelsen uses the example of the vendetta, in which an entire family can be the target of reprisals for acts committed by one of its members. But he also mentions international law—"reprisals and wars"—in cases when a state or a people as a whole is sanctioned for an international crime committed by one of its bodies.

It is striking that Kelsen doesn't treat collective responsibility and individual responsibility as two institutions, two equivalent and imaginable options, or two possible ways of organizing the law. On the contrary, he treats the transition from one to the other as evidence of progress and a symptom of modernity.

Kelsen presents the notion of individual responsibility as obvious, a fact that rationally imposes itself. As a result, he associates all other mechanisms with "feeling," "spontaneity," a "flaw," or lack of development. The idea that an act can be assigned to a collective body strikes him as a primitive notion associated with immediate and irrational impulses: "Collective liability is a characteristic element of *primitive* legal orders and is closely connected with *primitive* man's collectivistic thinking and *feeling*. Because of the *lack* of a sufficiently strong ego consciousness the primitive man identifies himself so much with the members of his group that he interprets any significant deed of a group member as a deed of 'the group'—as something that 'we' have done, and he therefore claims the reward for the group in the same manner as he accepts the punishment of the whole group." Modern law overcomes those flaws. It is liberated from erroneous and primitive feelings and targets the "sole" and "true" authors of acts: "Individual liability prevails if the sanction is directed exclusively against the delinquent—the one who by his behavior has committed the delict."[1]

Kelsen believes that modern law reflects something akin to an immediately given reality. Rationally, we are convinced that for every act there is a singular author, the delinquent, and that he or she alone must be held responsible. Any other system is considered blind to this "given": sanctions (or rewards) must be directed against the so-called author of the act.

FOR A HISTORY OF PERCEPTIONS

There is, however, a history of perceptions and a politics of vision. This is why it is legitimate to question the institution of *individual* responsibility: is it as obvious as it appears? Isn't it, on the contrary, dependent on a certain construction of reality? Aren't there other ways to think about what happens in the world, what happens to us, and the causes—ways that aren't necessarily antagonistic but possibly complementary? To speak more plainly: can't we consider individual responsibility and collective responsibility as two frameworks,

---

1. Hans Kelsen, *Pure Theory of Law*, trans. Max Knight (Clark, NJ: Lawbook Exchange, 2005), 122 (emphasis added).

one as fictional or artificial as the other? Neither is a reproduction of reality. Both are ways of constructing it. This clears the path for a questioning of the meaning and function of the justice system. Can't we describe what happens to us differently, take responsibility for it differently, and finally codify it differently? Can another ethics of perception, apart from an individualizing one, be envisaged?

A little-known work by the French sociologist Paul Fauconnet offers one of the most powerful and original analyses of responsibility and, more generally, of the frameworks that organize the ways in which we view the world and understand what happens within it.[2] His study, moreover, constitutes an important demonstration of the destabilizing force of sociological thinking when it is used to tackle theoretical problems. Using sociological analysis, Fauconnet radically challenges our ways of thinking and of constructing reality. He forces us to step back from who we are and imagine that other modes of social, political, and judicial organization are possible and imaginable. In *Responsibility*, a text characterized by its antinaturalism and integral constructivism, Fauconnet claims to be resolutely antifoundational, or, rather, he shows the antifoundational character of sociological thinking when deployed to its full extent. As a result, sociology appears to be a more artificializing discipline than Kelsen's theory of law. Sociology, rather than law, has the capacity to artificialize reality. Contrary to what one may think, and what is often said about the abstract character of legal science, sociological reasoning may in fact be more capable of problematizing reality than the law.

Designating a person as someone who must be punished constitutes a "fact of responsibility." Fauconnet analyzes these "judgments of responsibility" as institutions, narratives, and worldviews. Every society has rules that organize the way in which an entity, being, or

---

2. See Paul Fauconnet, *La Responsabilité* (Paris: Alcan, 1920).

group comes to be considered the "symbol" of a crime and therefore the "subject" to which a punishment must be applied—meaning framed as the "author" or "cause" of the act in question and thus as "responsible."

Fauconnet uses all the sociological or anthropological data at his disposal to reveal the variability of reactions to crime, meaning the facts of responsibility according to different contexts and time periods: sometimes these "facts" can target things, animals, and children, and sometimes only adults; sometimes they are focused on abstract entities, as well as spirits or ghosts.

What is essential for every society, be it "traditional" or "modern," is the ability to designate someone or something as a "sign," in other words, as a "being who/that can be substituted for the crime": the "destruction" or "punishment" of the symbol "replaces the destruction of the crime" and allows for expression of the collective censure of the infraction."[3]

The designation of the responsible subject can follow specific rules, but it can also occur randomly. Fauconnet cites, for example, observations made by anthropologists in Dagestan studying vengeance systems that are "not oriented in the least," notably the "first comer" vendetta: "In the event of a death of unknown cause, the deceased's family gathers before the mosque, declares one person at random to be the murderer, and then takes vengeance on him."[4] Fauconnet also notes that in certain societies in Australia, after burying the deceased, members of his or her clan carefully sweep and level the surface of his or her grave, after which the "first ant that crosses over it indicates the direction of the tribe responsible for the person's death."[5]

---

3. Ibid., 233–34.
4. Ibid., 235.
5. Ibid., 236–37.

Facts of responsibility can target entire groups (this would be the system of collective responsibility, as incarnated perfectly by the vendetta) or a lone individual (the system of individual responsibility).

Contrary to what one might think, Fauconnet's book doesn't focus primarily on the notion of "responsibility" or on the meaning of said notion. Rather than analyzing the concept as such, he focuses on the *direction* of responsibility. His study constitutes a critical investigation into our ways of seeing the world and interpreting the origin of what happens and what happens to us: Who can be held responsible for what? What is the source of whatever is affecting me? How do I think about the origin of the injuries I sustain? What are the causes of events that occur and that concern me?

Fauconnet rejects the idea that individual responsibility constitutes an objective and self-evident mechanism: the idea that an entire group can be held responsible for an action committed by one of its members cannot be seen as an aberration, an absurdity, or willful blindness. Individual responsibility and collective responsibility represent two equally valuable modes of perception, meaning that both are equally "artificial" or "arbitrary" and therefore equally conceivable. Why? Because, according to Fauconnet, the judgment of responsibility is a "synthetic" judgment. There is no direct, obvious link between a crime—or an act in general—and the responsible party:

> A given representation of a crime does not automatically allow for the emergence of a criminal. The orientation of the punishment is somewhat indeterminate: initially directed against the crime, it rebounds around it; its nature does not force it to strike in one place rather than another. The responsible party appears as the symbol of the crime; a bridge is erected between it and the crime,

leading the punishment from one to the other. But *crime and responsible party* nonetheless remain two heterogeneous terms. The patient is treated like the representative of the crime. But that ability to represent the crime had to have been conferred by a judgment. And within that judgment lies the fact of responsibility. The choice could have been different. Nothing in the collective representation of a crime, nothing in the need to punish it, necessarily implies that choice. Accusation and attribution, punishment and attribution are distinct operations.[6]

The apparatus of individual responsibility appears obvious to us. But that stems from the fact that we are entangled in a power apparatus that prompts us to construct a narrative of events in the form of a judgment of causality that leads from a single agent to an act—that prompts us, in other words, as soon as an act is committed, to establish that a single individual is its causal agent and to seek to identify this individual: an individual has caused the act. He or she is responsible. What's important here is that this narrative, story, and judgment of causality doesn't precede, despite appearances, the judgment of responsibility. It results from it. It's not because X caused the act that we consider him to be responsible; it's because of the apparatus of individual responsibility at work in societies such as our own that we construct a causal scenario leading from an individual to an act. In groups that have a tradition of assuming collective responsibility, a different narrative is constructed, one that identifies traits unique to the social group (its outlook, functioning, values) as the causes of the act in question.

The fact that we talk about so-and-so's responsibility for such and such an act cannot be explained by the existence of an objective causality. On the contrary, it is the spontaneous interiorization

---

6. Ibid., 240 (emphasis added).

of a collective or individualizing vision of the world that determines the representations that we set in motion and the way in which we construct this or that entity as the cause of a given event. *Causes and the narratives that support them are, in fact, effects.* In other words, it's possible to construct multiple narratives of events and actions, of who caused them, and who or what is responsible. These narratives are all legitimate. And no fact of responsibility is more rational than another, since any attribution of responsibility constructs the very causality (between an agent or entity and an act) it claims to observe.[7]

Fauconnet's work forces us to relate differently to something that appears self-evident. It denaturalizes or renders artificial the apparatus of responsibility. There is nothing obvious or inherent about the matter of my or someone else's responsibility or about the establishment of a causality link between an act and an actor. No system of responsibility is more real or genuine than another: designating a responsible party, passing judgment, and imposing sanctions are operations that depend on symbolic systems. Tying an act to groups or individuals, to collective structures or to an individual intention, reflects two possible ways of constructing reality and of what occurs in each of our lives.

In *The Imperative of Responsibility* Hans Jonas also underlines the fundamentally artificial nature of the apparatus of responsibility. The existence of "responsibility" is "conditioned" on the existence of a "causal power": a subject must be causally linked to an action to be held responsible. But that determination, notes Jonas, is formal. *It always comes from the outside.* A subject is *held* responsible. In other words, the notion of responsibility is linked to the question of how a vision of "causal action" comes to be imposed

---

7. Ibid., 222–23.

and how it establishes the subject as the individual we call to account. And if responsibility comes from the outside, there lies the proof that it is an institution exterior to the subject, one that is variable and therefore interchangeable—just like the system on which it rests.[8]

The strength of Fauconnet's argument comes from his use of sociological reasoning as an instrument to artificialize and problematize: the causal narratives that we construct are embedded within specific and transformable apparatuses, such that sociology can allow us to challenge our modes of perception and experiment with the possibility of looking at the world differently: "Punishment gravitates towards the crime. It is only because it cannot reach it that it rebounds onto a substitute for the crime. In that second stage, it can take many different directions. Nothing, it appears, constrains societies to narrowly delimit the circle within which they will choose the being who will serve as the substitute for the crime and become the object of the punishment's application. The relationship between symbol and symbolized thing is entirely undefined. Only the mind who establishes it perceives it and holds it to be valid."[9] Adopting a sociological perspective and recreating mechanisms of judgment thus leads us to accept the idea according to which "all beings are apt to eventually play the role of the responsible party."[10]

This denaturalization and artificialization of the apparatus of responsibility allows Fauconnet to conclude with a critical reflection in what are the book's most inspiring pages. He begins with the foundations of sociology: if it is true that something like society exists, that we are all formed by our relationships and the social

---

8. Hans Jonas, *The Imperative of Responsibility: In Search of an Ethics for the Technological Age*, trans. Hans Jonas with David Herr (Chicago: University of Chicago Press, 1984), 90–91.
9. Fauconnet, *La Responsabilité*, 234.
10. Ibid., 224.

groups to which we belong, then we must accept the idea that we are all implicated in what happens to each and every one of us. Expressing such an idea does not mean taking a revolutionary or even radical or crazy position. It simply draws necessary conclusions about the existence of the social world. Denying the validity of this proposition would be equivalent to denying the very idea of society. But the idea that we are all implicated in the world forces a radical conclusion: "All society, men and things, should always be responsible for all crimes."[11] It would therefore be easy to imagine a "virtually unlimited" responsibility, which would apply to every member of society for everything that happens within it.

Using the idea of society and reciprocal involvement to deduce the possibility of a virtually unlimited responsibility allows us to adopt a new perspective toward modern law and the individualization of the institution of responsibility. Questioning the criminal justice system requires unearthing the reasons why, when confronted by an event or act, we feel the need to identify, singularize, and judge rather than understand, generalize, and politicize: what purpose is served by an individualizing perception of events and the attribution of responsibility to singular subjects? Why create guilty subjects? What is the meaning of the system of judgment and of responsibility?

The primary function of individualizing modes of perception may not necessarily be to punish "responsible parties" and them alone. In fact, it's overwhelmingly a question of *not punishing everyone else*. This offers each of us the ability not to feel responsible for what occurs in the world. The objective is to allow us to establish ourselves as irresponsible subjects and to ensure that responsibility for the actions of one individual are not attributed to the group to

---

11. Ibid., 331.

which he or she belongs—meaning to everybody: "Irresponsibility is the rule, responsibility is the exception."[12] The function of the criminal justice system is therefore to relieve us of our responsibility by individualizing the system of law and punishment. The French criminal code's famous article 121-1, which formalizes the principle of individual responsibility—"no one is criminally liable except for his own conduct"—mustn't, in this sense, be uniquely understood as a protection that gives everyone the certitude that he or she won't be reproached for someone else's actions. If we adopt Fauconnet's perspective, we can see that its function is above all to defend us from the unconditional responsibility that potentially threatens to descend upon us. In short, it allows us to escape collective responsibility: no one should feel responsible for the actions of others.

POSSIBILITIES

Fauconnet's study has a tendency to limit itself, and by the end it loses its radicalness. Fauconnet essentially grafts a historical framework onto his sociological analysis of different systems of judgment and responsibility: *the history of modernity is the history of the increasingly large hegemony of individual responsibility to the detriment of all other systems.* Based on this approach, it is impossible to challenge or question individual responsibility, on either a theoretical or practical level. The apparatus of individual responsibility, in his view, is called for by the contemporary social order. Fauconnet thus expresses a "law of the evolution of responsibility": formerly collective and transmissible, responsibility becomes personal and individual.

Here, the individualization of responsibility is viewed as a consequence of the social division of labor, the diversification of society, and the strengthening of the state. The history of responsibility followed the history of individualization. It became part of the es-

---

12. Ibid.

sential dynamic of modernity identified by Durkheim and that consists of affirming a subject's autonomy in relation to the groups to which he or she belongs. This sociological and historic process was supposedly further reinforced by political and legal mechanisms, meaning the birth of the modern state: the state establishes and institutes individual rights and monitors their application. That is why there is no contradiction between the state and the individual. The state institutes individual rights in order to undo the hold of partial, local groups on their subjects, groups that rival the state's legality and hegemony: "The state is the great adversary of the vendetta and of collective responsibility. In order to be formed, it must weaken the close ties between individuals and families. Its battle against collective responsibility is one specific aspect of its fight against the autonomy of domestic groups. It emancipates the individual and isolates him or her at the same time. Contrary to what we might expect, the increase in individual freedom first brings about a lessening of responsibility. For the liberated individual is no longer responsible for anything but his personal actions. He escapes collective responsibility."[13]

THE MEANING OF THE SOCIAL STATE

Even if Fauconnet was right, and even if modernity were indeed linked to a process of the individualization of responsibility, it wouldn't mean that we are obligated to accept his conclusions. It's possible to apply his analyses to a political usage and question the perceptual frameworks that undergird the system of judgment as we know it. And fortunately, history is not as linear as it appears. It would be wrong to relegate all conceptions of nonindividual responsibility to the premodern past—as if living in the present necessarily means living in the era of individual responsibility.

---

13. Ibid., 334–35.

Granted, in the domain of criminal justice the notion of individual responsibility looms like an unsurpassable horizon. We can no longer imagine calling it into question. Holding a group or collective entity responsible for an act, and suggesting the possibility of *not* identifying someone as a causal agent and potentially responsible, and therefore allowing for the possibility of *not* judging, seems inconceivable. Yet the development of the modern state didn't follow a single, unique path. There are domains in which modernity has consisted, on the contrary, in moving away from individual responsibility toward a collective perception of phenomena, following a movement that is the reverse of the one outlined by Fauconnet: I am speaking of the social state.

I want to quickly clarify that the social state and its foundations don't interest me as such. Instead, I'd like to use them as instruments that can allow us to problematize questions of fault, guilt, and reparation in a different way. The social state is an apparatus whose constructing principles give us the opportunity to reflect on the way in which we can construct narratives of what occurs in the world, for which we can attribute blame and for which we, in certain domains, already assign causes of events differently than is the case in the field of criminal justice and the treatment of delinquency. This allows for a more nuanced understanding of the system of judgment.

Pierre Bourdieu's lectures about the state at the Collège de France are conducive for this type of reflection about the issues and concerns of the social state. Granted, Bourdieu was unclear or hesitant at times, making it difficult to know if he was talking about the state in general, the modern state as it appeared in the nineteenth century, or the social state/welfare state. He uses all three terms. My understanding, however, is that we should perceive his text as a reflection on the foundations of the social state, meaning about social security. The fundamental idea defended by Bourdieu is that of a link between social theory and the social state. Sociology offers a construction of reality in terms of the collective and solidarity, which is why its emergence played an essential role in the construction of the social state. The latter's establishment was bolstered by ideas of "the social," "the public," and "the collective." The social sciences go hand in hand with the construction of a philosophy or mind-set congruent with the idea of the welfare state. The welfare state could only emerge and take hold at the end of the nineteenth century because the social sciences had symbolically made possible its advent.

The essential stakes underlying the emergence of the state in the nineteenth century are the approaches to questions of fault and responsibility: Whose fault is it? Who is responsible? The state was born from a new way of thinking about those questions. Spontaneous thought individualizes: it seeks culpability in actions and their motivations and attributes to agents viewed individually the responsibility for what happens to them. Sociological thought, in contrast, socializes. It rejects categories of fault or intent. It rejects the representation according to which singular acts can be isolated from each other and explained individually by local reasons. On the contrary, those acts invariably express a collective tendency beyond their control. Events and actions must be considered the actualization of a potential rooted in social and collective structures—such that the individual who is their agent is not their cause.

Sociology thus proffers another vision of "responsibility" (for now I'm maintaining that designation, but later we will examine whether this field can in fact co-opt the notion of responsibility) that is collective, not individual, and that is to be found in the systems of relationships within which individual agents exist. The sociologist substitutes "a system of complex factors, whose weight must be evaluated, for an explanation in terms of *direct responsibility*, imputable to a free individual."[14] Sociological and social thought challenge the individualistic logic incarnated by liberalism—and today, according to Bourdieu, by neoliberalism—and which leads to the state's abdication and withdrawal through the creation of the free and autonomous individual responsible for his or her own fate.

Bourdieu cites several examples of symbolic revolutions that transformed the perception of certain realities, situated them in collective rather than individual logics, and thus made possible their treatment as social issues. He starts with illness and disease, which, once considered in terms of collective risk and public interest rather than negligence and fault, led to the creation of health insurance, a system in which common ailments are viewed as the consequences of social risks rather than the results of individual choices.

But the strongest and most pertinent examples are workplace accidents, equivalents of which can be found in most legal systems. These used to be seen as the result of a worker's negligence, weakness, or lack of discipline. At the end of the nineteenth century they were reclassified by French law as the "result of a collection of [objective] factors that can be controlled by preventative measures."[15] Rémi Lenoir published an important article describing the symbolic fight over workplace accidents, which pitted those who saw them as a mistake attributable to workers against those for whom they represented a risk tied to material structures and working conditions and for which responsibility should be collectively assumed: "If the idea of a workplace accident is so obvious nowa-

---

14. Pierre Bourdieu, *On the State: Lectures at the Collège de France, 1989–1992*, ed. Patrick Champagne, Rémi Lenoir, Franck Poupeau, and Marie-Christine Rivière (Cambridge: Polity, 2014), 364.
15. Ibid.

days, it is undoubtedly due in part to the legal and financial system implemented by the law of April 9, 1898, which situated the notion of objective responsibility in relation to the risk inherent in the material conditions of industrial work (machines, tools, raw materials, etc.)."[16] Here it is clear that this fight is not only symbolic; it leads to very different tangible consequences: in one case the worker is responsible for the mistake and must bear the costs of his injuries, whereas in the other he is insured against the risk and harm done to him and that he causes.

With his history of the birth of the social state, Pierre Bourdieu intended to assert that there is a theoretical dimension to the construction of the state. The state isn't an institution whose genesis and form are uniquely rooted in political, administrative, or economic logics. The state as we know it wouldn't have been possible without the establishment and circulation of new ways of thinking and seeing. It presupposes a relationship to and vision of the world. In return, its existence helps to reinforce a certain perception of reality and society. The state is not only a material given; it's also an idea—or better, a kind of institutional concretization of a prior symbolic revolution. This goes to show the extent to which the intellectual and theoretical battles that affect our self-representations are political from the start.

The state is a complex, incoherent, and contradictory institution. Not all of the domains in which it acts and intervenes share the same history or reflect the same logic. That is why a universally "anarchistic" position doesn't make much sense—criticism of one aspect of the state often incorporates values that guide other state practices.

The penal state and the social state are two organizational models attached to two contradictory perceptual models: individ-

---

16. Rémi Lenoir, "La Notion d'accident du travail, un enjeu de lutes," *Actes de la recherche en sciences sociales*, no. 32–33 (April–June 1980): 80, 82.

ual responsibility and objective responsibility. They are two institutions rooted in theoretical constructions, two possible ways of producing reality, and two conceivable narratives of events. In the domain of criminal justice, modernity has been powered by the individualization of the system of punishment and judgment, but in the social domain it has operated, on the contrary, via the "collectivization" of phenomena. On the one hand, the social state rests on a sociological vision: what happens to each of us is rooted in collective trends that manifest through us. On the other hand, the penal state operates via individualization, that is, by establishing individuals as causal agents.

The fact that these two extremes exist shows that, *already*, within the current legal and political reality, it is *possible to wrest the social world from the framework of individual responsibility and construct events and actions differently*. That is why the example of industrial accidents is so interesting. It allows us to grasp how the transition from an individualizing narrative to a structural narrative led to the decriminalization of a worker's actions.

SPECIFICITY

Before continuing, I want to underscore that, by exposing the existence of an antagonism between the principles of the social state and those of the penal state, I am breaking with a vision of the former that the vast majority of political philosophy or liberal—or social-liberal—theories tend to propose and that, consequently, empty mechanisms of social security and collective insurance of their radical implications.

The liberal tradition effectively tries to propagate a vision of the social state that conserves the individual values on which that tradition's reasoning is built. As a result, it is not unusual to observe that redistribution is intended to increase the capacities or capabilities of social actors. We find this in works by John Rawls and Amartya Sen, and it is a reasoning already visible in Friedrich Hayek's *The Road to Serfdom*. From this perspective the social state provides everyone with a kind of minimum, allowing each of us to become a responsible individual. Here, social logic is conceptualized as a condition of penal logic: aid, insurance, and assistance measures protect individuals against the primary "risks" in life, thanks to which they can largely avoid poverty or need and can determine their own existence. Because they are fully insured, they are fully responsible. Within this framework the social state almost legitimizes the criminal state and in any case becomes complementary to it: sanctioning individuals is all the more legitimate because they no longer have the excuse of being in need, for the state has assured them a certain level of capability.

In fact, such a perception prevents us from understanding the unprecedented, specific, and unique elements of the social state. The notion of the welfare state relies on an invalidation of the problem of the individual, and of individual responsibility, in favor of a socialization, objectification, and collectivization of problems: what happens in the world at a given moment is not the act of an individual but the actualization, in a precise location, of a collective force, a trend, or a risk tied to the social and material structures in which we are all immersed as long as we live in a society. As a result, it's society, and not such and such an individual, that is collectively and objectively behind what happens. A workplace accident or a disease is not the "fault" of the individuals to whom they befall but the consequence of a social risk to be assumed and resolved collectively. For that matter, how can we ignore, in examples such as pregnancy and maternity, the extent to which the construction of such occurrences as collectively insured social risks constitutes an artificial apparatus and a narrative—a victory of sociological and political reasoning, and of generosity, over spontaneous perception in terms of individual choices, personal responsibility, and therefore of nonassistance? Indeed, other victories in other domains, which undoubtedly clash with current spontaneous perceptions, cannot be ruled impossible.

AN INDIVIDUALIZING NARRATIVE

Saying that there is a penal state and a social state, and that each relies on contradictory theoretical dimensions and perspectives, means that each of these conceptions is forced to address and negotiate with the possibility of the other. These two modes of construction cannot assert themselves without denying and rejecting the other. In other words, in the same way that the construction of the social state rests on a refusal to think in terms of individual causality, and therefore of fault, the penal construction of reality rests on a rejection of sociological and structural analysis.

But, as one would imagine, expressing that conflict and antagonism doesn't equate to maintaining that a sociological point of view must lead to arguing for, say, the abolition of courts or any criminal justice system. Such a proposition would be pointless and absurd. A sociological perspective does, however, allow us to become aware of everything that we implicitly assume and suppress in the act of judging. A social critique of the logic of the penal state allows for an understanding of the system of judgment in terms of its positivity, foundations, and functions; therefore, it allows us to see how it belongs to a more general economy of power. It also forces us to ask a question: are we comfortable with what happens in the courtroom?

Hannah Arendt's notions of responsibility, judgment, and guilt reveal the extent to which any operation of judgment requires, as the condition for its very existence, an act of denial, which consists of relegating contextual elements and social forces to the background in order to attribute blame for an event or action to a single agent. Arendt, of course, reflected at length on the idea of collective responsibility in relation to Nazism, and notably Adolf Eichmann, as well as racial segregation in the United States. And I am aware that it is difficult to engage in discussion of her texts given the traumatic, complex, and overwhelming nature of her subjects.

Arendt aggressively challenged the idea of "collective responsibility"—or "collective guilt." Granted, she didn't completely dismiss this idea and acknowledged that it was possible to imagine the idea of a political responsibility: insofar as I belong to a political community, I am de facto responsible for acts committed in my name by the nation or government that represents me. According to Arendt, we can escape that political responsibility "only by leaving the community."[1]

But Arendt immediately adds that this notion of collective, political responsibility can under no circumstances be confused with legal or "personal" responsibility. She aims to refute the argument that the existence of a political responsibility implies that it is impossible to judge individuals for their actions. She speaks of "misplaced feelings" when talking about Germans or white liberals who maintain that "we are all guilty" and therefore deduce guilt from the mere fact of being German or white.[2] According to Arendt, this

---
1. Hannah Arendt, *Responsibility and Judgment* (New York: Random House, 2003), 147–50.
2. Ibid, 150. Karl Jaspers discusses similar "political guilt" in *The Question of German Guilt*, trans. E. B. Ashton (New York: Fordham University Press, 2000).

type of thinking constitutes first a kind of "declaration of solidarity with the wrongdoers"[3] (what a strange argument!). But above all, this perspective stems from a confusion among politics, morality, and the law. Yes, Arendt does think that a responsibility of the political community exists—*but only as a moral responsibility*. Under no circumstances can it prevent the functioning of the system of judgment and of legal responsibility. This is because guilt is purely individual. It is based on acts committed by persons *independent of any context or any reference to a system in which individuals are or were immersed*. Arendt states this explicitly: the judicial system, *as a matter of principle*, ignores arguments of a collective nature. This is why the idea of collective responsibility can never be used to counter the law.

In other words, the construction of a legal apparatus presupposes the relegation of anything that forms the general backdrop in which individuality is embedded. Criminal justice requires that we break with socializing and politicizing modes of thought. Arendt writes this conclusion in the form of a eulogy: "It is the undeniable greatness of the judiciary that it must focus its attention on the individual person, and that even in the age of mass society where everybody is tempted to regard himself as a mere cog in some kind of machinery.... The almost automatic shifting of responsibility that habitually takes place in modern society comes to a sudden halt the moment you enter a courtroom. All justifications of a nonspecific abstract nature ... break down."[4]

Arendt thus highlights and approves of the fact that, in a court of law, any invocation of a system, historical trend, or social environment is stripped of value. Justice judges "individual persons." Evoking the case of Eichmann, she emphasizes that a function-

---
3. Arendt, *Responsibility and Judgment*, 149.
4. Ibid., 57–58.

ary cannot hide behind the fact that he was obeying hierarchical orders: "If the defendant happens to be a functionary, he stands accused precisely because even a functionary is still a human being, and it is in this capacity that he stands trial." She continues:

> Hence, the question addressed by the court to the defendant is, Did you, such and such, an individual with a name, a date, and place of birth, identifiable and by that token not expendable, commit the crime you stand accused of, and Why did you do it? If the defendant answers: "It was not I as a person who did it, I had neither the will nor the power to do anything out of my own initiative; I was a mere cog, expendable, everybody in my place would have done it; that I stand before this tribunal is an accident"—this answer will be ruled out as immaterial.[5]

Arendt's argument has the merit of clarity and honesty. It, in fact, elucidates the criminal justice system's founding principles and conditions of possibility: to pass judgment, we must isolate singular existences and conceive of criminal acts as an empire within an empire. Social and political analyses must be interrupted or, in any event, sidelined. The deployment of justice entails the rejection of any perceptions in political, sociological, or structural terms; the relevance of those elements must be denied for "justice" to be dealt, for a trial and then a judgment to occur and have meaning.

ACTION

It's clear why a trial is not, first and foremost, an institution in which we investigate, establish what happened, and then judge. It's an action. A trial occurs in the sphere of representations. It is a moment of symbolic violence during which a nonsociological and even anti-

---

5. Ibid., 30–31.

sociological perception of the world is established. Criminal justice is a rite of depoliticization, dehistoricization, and desocialization.

When one observes a trial, one sees that judges endlessly repeat, in order to justify their questions, that "to judge is to understand." Oftentimes, they appear quite proud of this moving phrase. But they should be saying just the opposite: the act of judging is based on not understanding the facts in their entirety. Criminal justice is based on an atomistic vision of reality. The system of judgment and individual responsibility can only function if all reasoning about social causalities, collective structures, or historical logics has been set aside.

The analysis of a trial must concentrate on the operations through which it invents and fabricates its own subject matter: a trial is a mechanism through which the repressive state apparatus institutes a certain vision of the world and denies the external world, which is nonetheless there, in front of the judges, if only in terms of the social background of the individuals who appear, which demonstrates the extent to which social logics determine what is illegal.

My objective is to recreate how reality should be constructed and represented when we want to judge and in order for us to be able to judge. In other words, the events taking place in French courtrooms provide an opportunity for me to reflect on the logic at work in any system that aims to judge and punish and, furthermore, to deconstruct the functioning of that logic, which imposes itself on us, takes hold of us, and which we ourselves, quite often, enable.

REFUSE TOTALITIES

The criminal justice system's construction of reality is first and foremost based on a refusal to think in terms of totalities. In the judge's eyes there is no social situation in which individuals are caught up and that determines their actions. The idea of an interaction whose frameworks are imposed on actors and that is deployed according to a unique and autonomous logic has no meaning. This perspective can be defined as analytic and antisynthetic: it only sees individuals who act in an atomistic manner. The logic of the criminal justice system (which determines and nourishes the punitive urge) fractures totalities in order to isolate individuals. It individualizes causality.

In October of 2010 I observed the trial of a Polish homeless man being judged for assault and battery causing an unintended death. The context was simple and common (this kind of trial regularly takes place in criminal courts): a fight between four particularly inebriated homeless men during which one died from blows he received and a fall.

Ultimately, any single member of the group could have been the victim of another. Any one of them could have fallen in the wrong way, been hit especially hard, and died. In other words, everything here indicates a logic of interaction and a group dynamic that should be taken into account to understand what happened.

But the logic of the criminal justice system prevents that kind of reasoning. It forbids and excludes proceeding in that manner. Perhaps it's necessary to state this differently: the very idea of judging, the notion that, in this collective action, there is *something to judge*, necessitates and presupposes disregarding the entire *context of interaction* in order to reconstruct reality differently. The trial eliminates this collective scene and this context of interaction. The act of judgment is only possible if one breaks social situations down into separate elements endowed with their own individualities and intent.

The testimony given by witnesses, the questions asked them, and the way in which arguments were made reveal how the logic of the criminal system subsequently reconstructed the scene in a completely different way—understanding it not as a fight involving four people but as a sum of individual, isolated actions, each in response to one another. The events in question were viewed as a sequence composed of singular and extricable characters, unfolding in stages—blow by blow—which allowed for an investigation whose function was to determine each participant's respective role. An entire analytical exercise was then undertaken to try to determine individual responsibilities: Who started it all? Who threw the first punch? The second? How? At what moment? How hard? Where? What reaction did it provoke? and so forth. In this attempt at a sequential reconstruction of a collectively produced action, the defendant's criminal record (in this case, he had already been convicted for violent acts) was one of the only elements used to support the charges, sketch a portrait of the protagonists, and thus ultimately declare who was guilty.

The very notion of considering this kind of situation in terms of individual responsibility and intent constitutes a very specific and arbitrary interpretation, which is clearly no more of a given than a sociological interpretation. It may even be less self-evident in this case (granted, not in every case, but here, yes). How can we not be struck by the violence at work in the way that the judicial system seizes on these kinds of acts, changes their meanings, and treats those whom it constructs as "actors"? No reference is made to the homeless way of life, the violence inherent to their milieu, alcoholism, and so on. All those elements are rejected and obscured, as if they were irrelevant. And clearly this kind of reasoning is not solely theoretical: the homeless defendant in this case was sentenced to five years in prison, one of which was suspended.

WHAT CONSTITUTES A LIFE

I am well aware that one could rather easily object to the argument that there is a fundamentally antisociological dimension to the penal state and the analytical passion that drives "justice." After all, the criticism of the judicial system's denial of collective forces may appear to be contradicted by the fact that, regardless of the trial at hand, attention is always paid to the defendant's life and personality.

The reconstruction of the defendant's history and personality is accomplished, depending on the criminal system, through testimony by the defendant himself or family members and friends and at times by character analysts and psychologists or psychiatrists. This biographical reconstruction is justified by the claim that it allows the court to "know" the person it will judge, to better understand him and his motives, to learn who he is and what he does. In other words, this moment is often presented as the fulfillment of a "human" justice that seeks to understand those being judged and not to reduce an individual to his acts alone.

The French system meets this need to reconstruct a defendant's life story in the form of an interrogation: after the trial begins, the presiding judge of the criminal court begins to question the defendant, not about the facts or his or her involvement in the crime but quite simply about the defendant's life and history. (Often, a character analyst also testifies about the defendant's life.)

I've always been struck by this moment when the accused is questioned: the simple fact of asking a defendant to talk about himself before bringing up his possible guilt, meaning the basis of his presence at court, tends to make it appear that his involvement in the case goes without saying, that is, to spread the idea that a link exists between the two—and therefore to implicate him.

The questions asked by the presiding judge always respect the same order and the same logic. The ways in which they are formulated and sequenced are interesting because they allow us to see how the state perceives and constructs an individual's life and what it considers important to "understanding" it—in short, what constitutes a life. They also reveal how there can be a nonsociological use of social categories: class, gender, ethnic group, and the like can be used within the framework of an antisociological line of reasoning.

"Life" is reduced to the successive occupation of positions, institutionally defined or not, that form the ritual stages of a biography. Where and when were you born? What was your father's profession? Is he still alive? What was your mother's profession? Is she still alive? Do you have brothers and sisters? Where did you go to school? What was your education like? When did you leave school? Why? What jobs have you held? Are you married? Do you have children? And finally, of course, have you already had run-ins with the law or served time in prison? Do you have a police record? Why? This sequence of questions prompts curt answers from the defendant, which are often limited to a "yes" or a "no."

But the most interesting part comes from seeing how a criminal trial treats and uses these collected biographical elements. They won't be used to determine social logics, conditioned behaviors, and lifestyles that could have led the defendant to become who he is and do what he did. Instead, they are used as elements that allow the court to understand his "personality." From that point on, knowledge of the defendant's history serves to conduct an operation of mystification during which the social world is never presented as such, in its different manifestations, as a cause or reason. It will only be presented in terms of its impact on the defendant. Here the cause-and-effect relationship is never thematized in any way. In other words, the justice system will attribute the "cause" of the criminal act to character traits, which should actually be viewed as consequences of social conditioning as *much as the act being judged*, meaning they exist on the same plane as said act.

I'd like to use the example of the trial of a Serbian homeless man who was also charged, in October 2014, for violent acts that caused an unintended death. After asking the standard questions about his trajectory, the presiding judge broached other aspects of the defendant's life, beginning with his temperament. She asked him if he loved to fight, if he agreed with the testimony given by people who described him as "bad-tempered," and if, as the Serbian police claimed, he was a gang member. She then asked the defendant about his relationship with drugs and alcohol (an obsession among judges): Does he drink? What? How often per day? Would he describe his consumption as excessive? And, after he responded "no," she insisted: "Not even from time to time?" "Yes," he answered. "Ah, you see!"

This is a classic example of the personality assessments or interrogations that occur during criminal trials. In nearly every case their purpose is to reconstruct the "defendant's character," his alcohol and drug consumption, and, quite often, his "relationship to work." These facts are treated as information about the defendant that will allow the court to grasp the reasons behind his actions.

But when judges bring up "temperament" or "alcohol consumption" as ways to understand the defendant and explain the act being judged, they are in fact engaging in a very specific operation. It's quite clear, for anyone who stops to think about it, that these phenomena are *manifestations of the defendant's way of life, just like the actions that brought him to trial.* In other words, they aren't causes. They're effects. They're not explanatory principles but, on the contrary, exactly what needs to be explained.

The attention paid to the defendant's character and history is a ruse of the criminal justice system. Even as this logic eases the conscience by claiming to "understand," it links the act being judged to a series of individual traits without ever evoking their objective causes or roots in actual social and political life. The criminal act is therefore spontaneously separated from the social, economic, and political context in which it occurred and in which actors were inserted alongside others. It is directly linked to the defendant's life and perceived as embedded within a series of behaviors displayed by the person being judged. The act in question is connected to the person on trial and to his life, not to the social structure in which that life story took form. In short, it is desociologized.

ENDOGENIZE

The exclusion of all sociological or political understanding that undergirds the system of judgment explains the prominence of psychological or psychiatric knowledge within the legal process. There is no system of judgment that fails to demand, at one point or another, the construction of a narrative of what happened and an explanation for the defendant's actions: why did this person commit this act? This explains the relationship between the system of judgment and psychiatry, psychology, or psychoanalysis. These domains support the system by providing the narrative elements essential to its functioning.

The need to construct a psychological narrative of reality in order to be able to pass judgment can take different forms according to the country. In certain systems it may take an informal and implicit form, in which case judges, lawyers, prosecutors, experts, and witnesses use psychiatric language and psychological concepts in an attempt to provide reasons for what happened and construct a narrative.

In France a psychiatrist and a psychologist provide official testimony at every criminal trial. The essential link between psychological or psychiatric discourse and penalization is therefore fully assumed. For that matter, this is why the French system is so interesting: it magnifies the psychic life of penal power as it is deployed in every modern legal system.

The testimony given by expert psychiatrists and psychologists probably represents one of the most intense moments of a trial. It certainly marks the sequence that garners the most attention: judges, jurors, and lawyers all seem to believe unfailingly in the truth of what the expert is saying; they are constantly looking out for explanations for the act they have to judge in order to understand any inconsistencies, puzzling elements, unconfessed motives, and the like. Psychiatrists take literal pleasure from this situation, positioning themselves as important people, as those who, during a trial, incarnate knowledge and understanding—a detail that is particularly loathsome when one knows that their testimony almost always paints a troubling portrait of the defendant and will therefore undoubtedly extend his or her sentence. The socially orchestrated reverence for expert testimony is all the more disturbing given that it suffices to have just a little critical distance to observe the deceptively scientific character of these testimonies, which quite often veil distressing statements with technical terms intended to intimidate less educated individuals.

The interlinking of psychiatry and criminal justice was at the core of Michel Foucault's thinking in the 1970s. In his lectures at the Collège de France, *Psychiatric Power* and *Abnormal*, and of course in *Discipline and Punish*, Foucault analyzes the metamorphoses of the criminal justice system and of the representation of the criminal from the end of the nineteenth century forward. One of the objectives guiding his thinking is to show the extent to which the eruption of psychiatric expertise within the judicial system contributed to a radical transformation of the representation and treatment of the criminal. This last is no longer viewed as a simple "offender," meaning an individual defined by what he has done. Psychological expertise imposes the idea that the crime is also, and perhaps even primarily, the manifestation of a perverse life, of deviant tendencies, and of immoral urges and inclinations, established notably in childhood. A crime can therefore no longer be reduced to a simple violation of the law but is instead a psychologically rooted behavior. The criminal is no longer viewed as a normal person, identical to other persons—he or she is constructed as a "distinct personality." In *Abnormal* Foucault states: "Expert psychiatric opinion allows the offense, as defined by the law, to be doubled with a whole series of other things that are not the offense itself but a series of forms of conduct, of ways of being that are, of course, presented in the discourse of the psychiatric expert as the cause, origin, motivation, and starting point of the offense. In fact, in the reality of judicial practice they constitute the substance, the very material to be punished."[6]

The historical importance of this apparatus is to have completely redefined the representation of the criminal and therefore the meaning of a crime. A crime becomes something more than just an illegal behavior; it is the consequence and manifestation of an irregularity in relation to ethical norms. "Expert psychiatric opinion makes it possible to constitute a psychological-ethical double of the offense. That is to say, it makes it possible to de-legalize the offense as formulated by the code, in order to reveal behind it its double, which resembles it like a brother or a sister, I don't know, and which makes it not exactly an offense in the legal sense of the term, but an irregularity in relation to certain rules, which may be physiological, psychological, or moral, et cetera."[7]

In other words, the emergence of psychiatry, of psychiatric power, adds a new layer to the divisions established by the law. The separation between lawful and unlawful is doubled with another set of meanings and now distinguishes between moral and

---

6. Michel Foucault, *Abnormal: Lectures at the Collège de France, 1974–1975*, ed. Valerio Marchetti and Antonella Salomoni, trans. Graham Burchell (New York: Picador, 2003), 15.
7. Ibid., 16.

immoral, normal and abnormal, and so on. The judicial system no longer deals with an "offender" but with a "delinquent." Criminality is no longer assessed from a legal perspective but from a psychological-moral one. In this sense psychiatric power creates a new kind of man, *Homo criminalis*, characterized by the fact that he can be defined by his life rather than his offense. This implies not only that it is impossible to understand him without knowing his history and way of life (the delinquent is not merely asked what he did but who he is) but also—and this is equally important—that, in a way, the criminal exists *before* his crime (and, possibly, outside of it), given that this act is simply the supreme manifestation of a preexisting psychological or moral disorder.[8]

Foucault emphasizes the extent to which this "psychologization" of criminality radically contributed to modifying the very function of punishment and the judicial institution. Rather than being solely intended to punish an act or force compensation, the criminal justice system becomes an apparatus that takes charge of and reforms the criminal. In this context the "abnormal" individual must no longer simply be punished in the penal sense of the word. He must be reeducated, corrected, and transformed. Psychiatry's reconceptualization of crime thus led to the establishment of a new type of power situated at the intersection of the medical and legal worlds: "normalization." This power clearly didn't come out of nowhere, all on its own; it represents one of the ways in which disciplines evolved into modern techniques to control and train individuals.

Foucault intends to show how psychological or psychiatric analysis contributed to constructing criminal material, meaning that to which punishment would be applied. He argues that psychological interpretation should not be viewed as an explanation

---

8. Michel Foucault, *Discipline and Punish*, trans. Alan Sheridan (New York: Vintage, 1995), 286.

of a set of facts but as a production of facts and their meaning: "Psychiatry does not really set out an explanation of the crime but rather the thing itself to be punished that the judicial system must bite on and get hold of."[9] And, according to Foucault, psychological interpretation creates first and foremost a barrier. It molds the image of the criminal into an "abnormal" personality that needs to be reformed and normalized.

Foucault's analysis is extremely important. It is indeed true that the universe of moral judgment saturates the criminal justice system, in perhaps quite a troublesome way. Psychiatric discourse situates the crime within a series of irregularities that must be corrected. Yet, at the same time, psychiatry serves, I believe, another, parallel, function: to give consistency to a vision of the world on which the system of judgment and punishment relies.

Psychiatry isn't principally aimed, as Foucault claims, at producing abnormal individuals, deviants, and delinquent personalities. I believe that its primary function is to substitute for and block all modes of sociological, historical, or political understanding. As Didier Eribon has shown, a radical antagonism exists between psychological knowledge and sociological knowledge, to the extent that the refusal to refer to the latter to construct a theory of the subject and the world obliges us to resort to the former. The refusal to think in terms of social forces external to the subject forces us to think in terms of internal drives and individual deviations.[10] In other words, "psychiatric knowledge" mustn't, as Foucault would have it, be viewed first and foremost as an identity-creating apparatus that binds the subject to himself and attributes to him a fixed essence that transcends his actions. It's above all a branch of knowledge at war with sociological knowledge—and against a social and

---

9. Foucault, *Abnormal*, 16.
10. See Didier Eribon, *Une morale du minoritaire* (Paris: Flammarion, 2015), 293–95.

political perspective—whose self-appointed task is to circulate narratives that provide an alternative to sociological ones while maintaining that what happens in the world is rooted in forces internal to the subject, not in the external, collective forces imposed on him in the same way that they may be imposed on us.

By definition, the psychological approach considers the individual to be a relevant entity of analysis. This is why it can uphold and be so easily integrated into the individualizing narrative of the world as constructed, for example, by the penal state. In order to judge, the justice system seeks the cause of an action in an individual. By endeavoring to associate an author with a crime, psychological and psychiatric discourse reinforces the state's construction of the world, which isolates individuals and links them directly to what happens in the social world.

In a sense the inflation of psychiatric discourse in the judicial world can be seen as a response to sociology's emergence and growing profile. It works to avert the destabilizing effects that such analyses might provoke. In any case this allows us to see that the discourse most radically critical of criminal justice may not be, as Foucault believed, that which, in opposition to the notion of a criminal "personality," reduces the criminal to his acts and eliminates all biographical elements. Rather, it is more likely the discourse that mobilizes the instruments and concepts of sociology, and thus proposes a sociological understanding of the defendant's history, childhood, and relationship with the world, rather than outright rejecting those concepts, as did Foucault.

In this respect one trial struck a particular chord with me: from October 17 to October 21, 2011, a fifty-four-year-old man was tried in Paris's assizes court for two armed robberies and illegal confinement in two Parisian jewelry shops, one in 2005 and the other in 2009. He admitted to the charges (video footage clearly identified him).

Here, there are all the makings of a classic sociological explanation of the defendant's trajectory in life. He was born into an extremely poor immigrant family. He grew up in Saint-Denis in rudimentary housing without water or electricity (the closest water source was located one thousand feet away). He had four brothers and four sisters; three of his brothers died, two of AIDS and one of alcoholism. Family conflicts, poverty, destitution, and so forth prompted him to leave his family and school at a young age, around sixteen. That's when a life interspersed with prison terms for theft, burglary, and robbery began.

This individual's actions could have been narrated by socializing and politicizing what happened, beginning with the question of the system of ownership, class relations, immigration (the defendant's father was Algerian and his mother German), unequal educational opportunities, and familial violence. But the criminal justice system demands an alternative narrative. It needs one in order to come to life, to exert its full powers, and to judge. So the deposition of the expert psychiatrist becomes the trial's key moment. His testimony essentially constructs the defendant's personality so as to make it lead inexorably to the crime, as if the crime has always already been there, dictated by fundamental psychic structures that, to be corrected, require reform and self-improvement and that bear no relation to economic and social structures. In effect, it is as if the robber's act cannot be perceived as that of a penniless individual seeking a way to make some easy money or as that of an individual more or less "professionalized" in this kind of activity.[11] The psychiatrist's job consists, on the contrary, of situating the robberies within

---

11. Edwin Sutherland introduced the notion of occupation and apprenticeship to the sociology of deviance. See Edwin Sutherland, *White Collar Crime* (New York: Holt, Rinehart and Winston, 1949). For a summary and analysis of different social theories of deviance see Albert Ogien, *Sociologie de la déviance* (Paris: PUF, 2012).

a series of *exclusively internal* psychological deviations. It is this internal confrontation experienced by the robber that is the supposed cause of his illegal actions, independent of any social factor.

The expert witness at this particular trial, Frantz Prosper, is well known. Prosper began his deposition by describing the defendant as a "paradoxical man": "He doesn't show the world who he is, deep down." He has a "capacity to appear different from what he is." Bringing up the defendant's childhood, the psychiatrist stressed the financial difficulties the former encountered and the extreme poverty in which he lived. That situation provoked a full-blown "obsession with precarity and with lack." That was the defendant's first major personality trait, according to the expert.

The second was explained as a reaction to that obsession: the defendant supposedly harbored a "fantasy of success" and spent his time imagining and claiming to be a different version of himself. He therefore created an image of himself as an "enterprising" and "dynamic" individual. That vision functioned as a "narcissistic compensation" and a "mythomaniacal auto-suggestion," making him an "immature" and "fragile" man, unable to "confront reality" but instead constantly seeking to "circumvent" and "escape" it.

The defendant's long criminal history was explained by a "tension." That tension had no objective reality but was an internal mental structure. His personality, in other words, was the combination of two conflicting attitudes: the realization of his social failure, on the one hand, and his fantasy of success, on the other. The defendant was characterized as "organized" between a "negative polarity of lack" and a "positive polarity of possession" that shaped his drive to commit crimes. To resolve this interior dilemma, the accused stole—and also, added the psychiatrist, worked out a lot.

The psychiatrist insisted that the defendant's criminal activities could under no circumstances be explained by his financial difficulties. The dilemma between lack and the desire to possess that characterized him was *entirely internal*. The psychiatrist refuted all social causality in order to effectively confine the defendant to a strictly psychological and interior dilemma. According to him, the "delinquent's" fundamental problem was his proclivity for "mythomaniacal auto-suggestion." The defendant spent his time telling himself: "I am not who I am." He was never content. He was structurally lacking something. He always wanted more. In other words, the "lack he feels isn't real. It's part of his psyche, the way he functions." To put a stop to his delinquent impulses, the defendant must therefore work to "improve himself" in order to learn not to refuse the reality in which he is immersed: "He needs to change his perception of reality and of what success is." The psychiatrist became even more explicit: "He has to be satisfied with what he is capable of achieving on his own. . . . He has to learn humility." In short, he has to accept his economic and social condition instead of experiencing it as a lack or as absence.

The psychologization of crime and the negation of the sociological vision of the world are one and the same thing. Psychiatric knowledge desocializes. It converts social forces into internal drives and denies the action of structural mechanisms (there is no dispossession, only a lack), unless they take the form of psychic mechanisms endowed with a certain degree of autonomy. We might therefore say that, in a sense, psychological knowledge endogenizes the social world. With this forceful blow it makes possible the system of judgment. The world more or less disappears. Everything that is external becomes internal. Crime is no longer the translation of a relationship to the world but the exteriorization of a relationship to the self.

REACT DIFFERENTLY

The system of judgment relies on a narrative construction of reality that is based on a threefold operation: refusing totalities, biographizing, endogenizing. These operations have a precise goal: produce a specific image of what occurs in the world, link events to individual histories, and render internal the social forces that affect us—in short, depoliticize our perception of the world. Once this individualization of the world has been accomplished, judgment can get underway: You have caused this. We must turn to you to redress what happened and to prevent it from happening again. You're guilty. You behaved badly. I will judge you.

EXCUSE: A BEAUTIFUL WORD

I am of course well aware that as soon as one proposes a social criticism of criminal justice or underlines the extent to which the system of judgment is based on operations that conceal social forces and collective contexts or structures, one finds oneself accused of providing "sociological excuses" for "criminals." That expression, which acts as quite the dissuasion, seems to designate a pitfall that threatens all discourse critical of justice and a trap that sociologists, at the risk of losing their credibility, should avoid at all costs when trying to understand or explain delinquent careers.

Many of those who write about crime feel compelled to preempt the possibility of their work being interpreted as offering "excuses" for the accused. One example in particular of this "anti-excuses" obsession has struck me in the last few years: a book by the journalist Gitta Sereny entitled *Cries Unheard: Why Children Kill: The Story of Mary Bell*. The eponymous subject is an eleven-year-old girl from England who killed (or, rather, was found guilty of killing, because doubts remain about her degree of involvement) two children aged three and four. The author became fascinated by this story and decided to investigate Mary Bell. She conducted long interviews with the young girl, her neighbors, and her acquaintances in an attempt to reconstruct Mary's family life, childhood, relationships with her neighbors and school friends, and living conditions.

Yet this endeavor, both necessary and important—the book is beautifully written—is regularly interrupted by the author's repetitive and compulsive assurances that her book should not be interpreted as giving "excuses" for Mary. She writes, for example, on page 9: "Not one word Mary Bell has ever said to me, not one word I have written, can be interpreted as an excuse for what she did." On page 22 she repeats: "I had always been convinced that [her childhood] had been even worse than her family had admitted to me, and I suspected that full knowledge of it could lead to an explanation for her terrible acts in 1968 [the year the murders were committed]."[1] And so forth.

I understand, of course, the rhetorical strategy behind this reiteration in the form of denial. It's intended to shield against the violent and malicious attacks that the sociological method can provoke when it tackles this kind of subject. But it's worth examining

---

1. Gitta Sereny, *Cries Unheard: Why Children Kill: The Story of Mary Bell* (New York: Metropolitan, 1998).

why it seems so impossible, unthinkable, or intolerable to use a sociological approach to reflect differently on the acts handled by the justice system through the mechanism of individual responsibility and to hinder our impulse to judge.

Indeed, I find it difficult to understand why the notion of excuse has been stripped of credibility, primarily because there is nothing unthinkable about finding excuses for an individual's actions. After all, the act of *"excusing" is a mechanism already present in contemporary criminal law.* As I demonstrated in the beginning of this section, the law shouldn't be considered as a system that simply establishes us as responsible for our actions. The grandeur of the modern state and criminal law stems, in fact, from its capacity to *create irresponsible subjects.* The state already accepts the idea that certain subjects may not be responsible before the legal system or that their responsibility can be diminished. Take, for example, the excuse of age, which reduces punishments for minors. But the same applies to defense arguments based on a defendant's "lacking" or "impaired" judgment: these psychological problems function as an excuse and allow for the diminishment of an agent's responsibility or even for him or her to be altogether absolved of responsibility.

In other words, the state has already instituted systems that excuse the accused. As a result, it's hard to see how there could be anything inherently illegitimate about resorting to that category—except that it appears that the state only considers as valid the excuses provided by psychologists and psychiatrists. But why should it be impossible to imagine a similar achievement for sociology? Why not use advances in this field to further develop the idea of criminal responsibility and to consider the practice of judgment differently? Isn't it precisely the state's role to allow for that kind of innovation? Would it really be so absurd to demand such a possibility?

This argument is all the more valid given that, ultimately, the most problematic element of the idea of excuse appears to be its tendency to present any acknowledgment of social forces weighing on agents as a "generous" act. But is it really the act of seeking excuses that is problematic? Isn't the fundamental refusal to imagine that possibility more troubling?

Earlier I mentioned the opposition between two possible narratives: the individualizing narrative and the collective narrative. That wording may give the impression of two equivalent apparatuses, equally artificial, between which we can choose. But that's not entirely correct. Social forces do exist. Objective determinations are real. This means that the repressive character of the system of judgment stems precisely from the fact that it forces individuals to respond to their actions according to a logic out of step with the logic of reality. The violence of the state comes, in part, from its negation and denial of the sociological vision of the world; therefore, there is nothing "generous" about wanting to reduce that initial violence even a little bit. Excusing doesn't reflect a principle of generosity but of reality.

In her critical analyses of the idea of collective guilt, Hannah Arendt maintains that the "grandeur" of justice comes from the fact that it isolates events, denies the relevance of contextual elements, and completely rejects the value of invoking structural forces at the moment when judgments of responsibility and culpability are being made: to judge means to judge individuals *abstracted from their environment*. But, one might retort, denying the existence of objective social forces doesn't stop them from existing or from playing and continuing to play a role. In the end we have to be harsh with Arendt and the way in which she conceived of her intellectual approach in this domain. What she describes as "grandeur" can also be considered an irrational and violent practice. For that matter, what are the relevance and legitimacy of a denial that acts as if what exists in fact does not? Isn't it strange to see an intellectual like Arendt, normally so compelling and original, endorse violent operations of mystification by evoking a so-called "evident necessity" to judge, a need for justice that is never questioned in itself? The intellectual's role consists of developing a line of reflection as far as it can go rather than suddenly stopping one's reasoning in the name of preserving established social rites. Arendt stops thinking when she enters a courtroom. Yet the theorist's function is not to protect social institutions, at all costs, as they were formed. It's to use analysis as an instrument to destabilize that which appears self-evident.

We shouldn't be afraid of the word *excuse* or of the consequences it engenders. Nor should we allow ourselves to be intimidated by the operations that have made the term so unappealing. Perhaps we could even set out to appropriate, claim, and reshape it into a positive term in the theoretical and political sphere.

In a text published in the French newspaper *Libération*, Didier Eribon talks about how progressive thinking has too often allowed itself to be defeated by attacks from conservative intellectual quarters, to the point of at times mirroring their viewpoints and vocabulary. He refers to the issue of "handouts" and the fact that, beginning in the 1980s in France, a large segment of the official Left began to include the idea of a "war against handouts" in its programs. Eribon retorted that, on the contrary, it should valorize a "beautiful word: assistance": "All it takes for my old anger to resurface intact is to remember the 2007 presidential campaign in which the socialist candidate's policy statement read, in the second line, that we should do away with the 'handout' society (what a horrible word!). But shouldn't a leftist project strive to develop and multiply systems of assistance (what a beautiful word!)?"[2]

In the same way, I'd like this book to be the starting point for a

---

2. Didier Eribon, "Voyous et fantômes," *Libération*, Dec. 6, 2009, www.liberation.fr/chroniques/2009/12/05/voyous-et-fantomes_597405.

counteroffensive in the domains of language and practice. We need to use another "beautiful word"—*excuse*—when countering criticism of sociological discourse. After all, wouldn't the elimination, in certain cases, of the overly rapid attribution of an act to an individual conscience, so as to factor in the collective determinations behind that act, represent the ultimate triumph of reason? We have here the outlines of a sociopolitical project that could allow for the introduction of greater rationality into practices of judgment and punishment in order to empty them of their ritual character, which often leads them automatically and remorselessly toward symbols that, regardless of the truth, satisfy a desire for expiation and order.

CONSTRUCT TOTALITIES

But it isn't enough when asserting a sociological perspective to merely insist on the role of social structures or collective histories in actions and to thereby challenge the perception of these actions as individualistic and the resulting impulse to judge. As important as that assertion may be, it tends to confine the social perspective to the role of providing some sort of new or supplementary thickness to the subdivision of reality enacted by the criminal justice apparatus. By intervening *after* the state's construction of reality, sociology would be reduced to a secondary position.

But on a deeper level a sociological line of reasoning should lead us to profoundly challenge the state's construction of reality and the divisions produced by the system of judgment, to reconfigure our perceptions, and to label what occurs in the world differently. The obligatory question for any critical analysis of judgment therefore becomes one of vision: What can be substituted for the vision of the criminal justice system? What would it mean to understand what happens to us differently and reorient our outlook? How can we produce another reality, explain events with other narratives, and consequently relate and react to them according to new forms and methods?

It's difficult to imagine what new perceptual principles might look like. But we can begin to do so using a text by Jean-Paul Sartre that offers a political critique of justice. In a lecture entitled "Justice and State" Sartre targets the criminal justice system. He wants to show that *judges are unaware, as a matter of principle, of the nature of the cases they are given to judge. They don't understand them*.[3]

Sartre invokes the trial of militant Roland Castro, who was accused of "assaulting an officer." He summarizes what happened: Activists and intellectuals (including Jean Genet, Michel Leiris, and Sartre himself) decided to occupy the offices of the CNPF (Conseil national du patronat français [National Council of French Employers]) to protest the deaths of five immigrant workers who had been asphyxiated by makeshift heaters that they had been using to warm themselves. The goal of this symbolic occupation, according to Sartre, was to "point out to the public the people who were truly responsible for these deaths": French employers.[4] Riot police intervened, rather violently, to remove the occupiers, some of whom were arrested. While trying to escape, Roland Castro allegedly shoved two officers, leading to his being charged.

Sartre uses this incident to reflect on the operations at work in criminal justice—or, more precisely, the conditions necessary for something like criminal justice to exist. For the judges, given the facts they had been provided, the problem was simple: did Roland Castro shove the officers or not? During the trial, that boiled down to the following question: were officers present or not at the door of the van from which Roland Castro had attempted to escape?

---

3. Sartre, Jean-Paul. "Justice and the State," *Life/Situations: Essays Written and Spoken*, trans. P. Auster and L. Davis (New York: Pantheon, 1977), 172–97.
4. Ibid., 69.

And, ultimately, the information the judges were eliciting from witnesses was this: were these two officers at that spot? This reduction of what occurred to the possible interaction between Castro and members of the riot police allowed the system of judgment to be deployed and this militant to be assigned responsibility in a potential case of violence against a police officer. But the fundamental condition of this system of judgment is clear: the refusal to consider the event in its totality. *The altercation between Castro and members of the riot police occurred within a larger context*, beginning with the violence of the police intervention against the occupiers, which, according to Sartre, could have justified Castro's escape attempt. But, more important, the question of *why* there was a confrontation between occupiers and police—of why militants and intellectuals occupied the CNPF headquarters—wasn't even asked.

What triggered the protest (of which the incident judged at Castro's trial was but one aspect) was the French employers' policy toward and treatment of immigrants, which took place with the government's complicity. Yet that detail was completely ignored in this case. The context of a broader dispute was rejected on principle: "The problem became very simple. Had there been, or had there not been, officers outside . . . and had Castro pushed them as he was getting out? This militant could just as well have been a thief or a drunkard arrested for disturbing the peace."[5]

In contrast to the individualizing logic of penality, reconstructing the context in its totality allows us to understand this altercation differently. It wasn't triggered by Castro's individual will but by management policies and the employers' relationship to immigrants, the death of several of those immigrants, and the desire to protest the living conditions forced on them—not to mention the

---

5. Ibid., 70.

riot police's intervention to protect CNPF headquarters. In short, a set of political, economic, and social factors was fundamentally "responsible" for the act being judged. Abstracting Castro the individual from that intricate context entailed the construction of a depoliticizing and desocializing narrative:

> But the judge wanted the whole truth concerning an infinitesimal incident: were these two men in such and such a place? *And none of us could understand why the event was not dealt with in its totality—that is, by starting with government and management policies.* To tell the whole truth about an infinitesimal instant is a pure contradiction. Truth develops over time. In a closed, limited instant, there can be no truth. But if the truth had been established, if the discussion had included the deaths of the black workers and the occupation of the CNPF, the trial would have been political. This was something which neither the government (and its representative, the prosecutor) nor the judge wanted. From that point on, the outcome was obvious: Castro was found guilty.[6]

Sartre's reasoning is part of a political context and a broader reflection on political trials. He wanted to show that by treating political events as if they were ordinary crimes, bourgeois justice helps maintain a capitalist and exploitative system. The justice system denies these events their strength, their dissenting significance, and thereby impedes awareness. It avoids recognizing demonstrations against state actions as political by recurring to common law. Accepting the political nature of those demonstrations would be tantamount to admitting the existence of an alternative to the liberal system.

Nonetheless, Sartre's argument is far from reducible to this context, and, in my opinion, it poses essential questions. Through its

---

6. Ibid., 70–71.

inventiveness and radicalness his analysis is the exact opposite of Hannah Arendt's approach, which I discussed earlier. Sartre demonstrates exactly how abstract and artificial the logic underlying the criminal justice system is and to what extent it opposes a political and social vision of the world: that logic constitutes a "truth." It isolates elements, and seeks antecedents, but it does so based on an ignorance of the totality of the situation it claims to understand. There is something beyond what the judge sees and isolates: a logic of totalities that escapes the gaze of the judicial system and imposes that a given act be inscribed within another narrative or story.

The legal system, in its construction of reality, isolates actions: it defines and views them independently of the circumstances in which they unfold, imposing a significance on them that may differ from that accorded by the actors involved. Acts are presented to magistrates and then judged in such a way as to strip them of all real meaning.

Where the law sees an altercation between a militant and a police officer, Sartre sees a battle against the treatment of immigrant workers by employers and the state. Sartre contrasts the criminal justice perspective with a political vision of totalities. In other words, he in no way aims to explain Castro's actions in sociological terms, to seek the social forces that would explain why he did what he did. Thinking in terms of totality means refusing the penal construction of reality in order to consider events, their significance, and the narrative behind them differently.

HISTORY OF VIOLENCE

Between October 31 and November 7, 2011, a trial was held in Paris's assizes court that asked exactly these types of questions. Three Indian men—once again, homeless—were summoned on charges of murder and attempted murder.

The entire trial revolved around the following question: what had happened three years prior at the Porte de Montreuil metro station? For the presiding judge, the lawyers, and the prosecutor the meaning ascribed to this question and the possible answers were obvious. This entailed asking whether the court was dealing with deadly assault, manslaughter, or murder, as the investigating judge insisted. Was there resentment between the protagonists, or were there issues of jealousy or debt? Did they know each other well? Or was it simply a fight between vagrants that ended badly? And based on that, of course: Who hit whom? How hard? Did they arrive on the scene armed?

After four days of arguments it was revealed that the descriptions of the events for which the defendants had been summoned had been exaggerated. One was acquitted, and the other two were convicted of voluntary aggravated assault causing an unintended death.

This case took place in a particular milieu populated by the hotchestnut vendors who divide Paris among themselves each winter, notably its metro exits. The fight that led to one man's death erupted in this very specific universe, composed almost exclusively of men, mostly of Indian origin, who sleep together under bridges and drink excessively every night (as many as five bottles per person). The trial gradually revealed the depth of the codependency among these men, some of whom lend others their carts and grills as needed, guard each other's spaces, provide chestnuts in exchange for a portion of that day's takings, and so forth.

Given this, what series of events was being represented by the altercation as understood by the criminal justice system? The court's construction of reality isolated this incident and sought out a category with which to describe it: the resulting system of problematization prompted the question of whether said incident was murder, manslaughter, or deadly assault. But sociology develops another perception. It problematizes this kind of altercation as an incarnation, or translation, at a given moment, of a totality in which mechanisms of economic dispossession, social poverty, homelessness, codependency, and unwanted proximity are all at work. What we should see in these "voluntary aggravated assaults causing an unintended death" is the form taken, at a given place, by a more general history of violence (to borrow the title of a novel by Édouard Louis).[7] A political interpretation of totalities allows us to deploy an observational language that gives a different name to what the criminal system reduces to and understands as a fight between vagrants. Therefore, we are not only explaining reality from a sociological basis but constructing another reality, designating what happens in a different way: where the penal state "sees" a murder, we should see the violence of a precarious existence, the violence of emigration and immigration, the violence of masculine sociability, the violence of the state, and the violence of economic marginalization.

WHAT SOCIOLOGY CAN DO

The criminal justice system should be understood as an apparatus and a power practice embedded within a more general political economy. The way this system seizes on what is real and constructs problems shapes our gaze and our relationship to what happens. Its mere existence validates and establishes a perception that leads us, when an event—assault, theft, what have you—occurs, to assign its cause to an individual. As a result, it suffices to punish that individual in order for the event to be deemed "closed" and for us to feel, as they say, that the lesson was learned.

---

7. See Édouard Louis, *Histoire de la violence* (Paris: Seuil, 2016). The novel explores how the enclosed space within which a theft, rape, and murder attempt occur constitutes a stage on which other more general forces emerge and shift, including the history of migration, class inequalities, and socialization during childhood.

We can understand the meaning of this system in two different ways, which are likely both true and complementary. First, we can maintain that the penal state strips us of a capacity for politicization. It teaches us to interpret events and actions that occur in the world as local and rooted in biographical trajectories and to therefore isolate them from historical mechanisms that not only cause and influence them but which they in fact—and this is even more important—incarnate and express at a given moment. In this sense the system of judgment activates diversionary operations that deflect our attention from the social logics from which singular acts stem—and thereby immunizes those logics from criticism.

The idea that the punitive apparatus serves to maintain order was affirmed by Michel Foucault. According to him, the criminal justice system aims to avert the threat of seditious masses and popular protests. It was formed in the context of a battle against popular uprisings in order to be able to control the chaos of war: it monitors; it punishes the slightest disruptions; it detains the most agitated individualities, thereby separating them from the dominated group; it creates a delinquent milieu removed from politics; it instills docile dispositions; and it divides the working classes into criminals and honest workers. Accordingly, the criminal justice system should not be understood (primarily) as a response to delinquency. It constitutes, before anything else, an "anti-seditious protection" in society: "The penal system–delinquency couple is an effect of the repressive system–seditious system couple."[8]

Personally, I have never found this rhetoric entirely convincing, haunted as it is by the vision of a perpetually simmering popular insurrection, which power desperately attempts to dismantle, slow down, or break apart. But it remains true that, at the same

---

8. Michel Foucault, *Théories et institutions pénales: Cours au Collège de France, 1971–1972* (Paris: Gallimard-Seuil, 2015), 102.

time, on another level, we can clearly describe criminal justice as an apparatus that prevents conflicts and favors the conservation of order. However, that function tends to be carried out through the intermediary of interference on the representational level: the system of judgment is a system of depoliticization. It inculcates categories—or reinforces perceptual frameworks—that prevent the politicization of what happens to us, divert our attention from structures, and, consequently, hinder our ability to problem-solve, mobilize, and protest. Our attention is drawn to individuals, and we are therefore prompted to feel the impulse to judge and punish.

But perhaps we can grasp the meaning of the criminal justice machine in an entirely different way and imagine that its very goal is to allow us to apply this depoliticizing treatment of the world. Through, and thanks to, that system, we give ourselves the means with which to disengage from what happens, to not suffer the consequences. The function of such an apparatus is therefore to enable us to avoid feeling called on when something occurs, to not feel involved or compelled to act to change things—and in this way to escape the unconditional responsibility that would threaten to strike us at any moment if we were to adopt a sociological vision of the world to the detriment of an individualizing one.[9]

Perhaps we've never taken sociology to the limit of what it can offer us. Perhaps we've never experienced the extent to which it incarnates a rupture with our ordinary ways of thinking. Sociology deconstructs the narrative that supports the state and juridical construction of the world, and it offers an alternative. That is why it represents a virtual power able to destabilize the edifice of criminal justice. The sociological perspective might thereby become a liber-

---

9. For more on the idea of an unconditional responsibility for what occurs in the world, tied to the interpellation and emergence of the other, see Judith Butler, *Parting Ways: Jewishness and the Critique of Zionism* (New York: Columbia University Press, 2013).

ating instrument with regard to the order of law and the system of individual responsibility.

Our challenge then becomes to reflect on the possibility of creating new narratives. That means reformulating what happens in order to develop a new awareness of reality that will prompt us to assign the cause of events not to individual agents but rather to collective logics rooted in concrete situations. We must question our urge to judge and orient our energy toward transforming political totalities rather than toward punishing individual actions, which are merely the occasional and local manifestations of those totalities. What would it mean to transform victims into rebels instead of plaintiffs?

The project of reconstituting collective logics rather than identifying responsible individuals is an ethical task. It requires a reconfiguration of our experience and, especially, of our relationship to politics and policing. At present, in my opinion, we are not conscious enough of what our use of political vocabulary betrays, particularly when we use a term like *politicization*: we think of the adoption of a political point of view of ourselves or events, and the construction of a political action, as something that *comes after*, a conquest, effort, or endeavor with respect to our initial perceptions and our common sense. But that is neither a given nor an inevitability. It results from our inclusion within a power apparatus that inculcates us with depoliticizing perceptual categories. If politics always implies that we undertake an act of politicization, isn't that the proof that we, in fact, maintain a nonpolitical relationship to the world? Sociology would force us to break with that inclination in order to experience what we might call an immediately political relationship to the world.

Were this to happen, the consequences would be much greater than we can imagine.

PART FOUR

THE SYSTEM OF PUNISHMENT

ACCUSE AND PUNISH

NEUTRALITY

Whenever we study an institution like justice, a collection of ideas, problems, and images emerges, invading and surrounding us, that largely dictate the form of the investigations possible. Culture is a space riddled with representations that shape our gaze and vision. Languages take hold, impose themselves, and predetermine even the very modes through which perspectives that claim to be critical are formed, if only to allow them to do just that.

In our imaginations, as in political or theoretical thought, the question of justice isn't associated solely with issues of judgment, responsibility, or the attribution of acts. It is also strongly linked to the problem of impartiality and independence, as well as to the aspiration to something akin to neutrality, universality, and objectivity—something that is, in a word, just. The idea of law refers to the construction of a system whose mission is to be equitable, meaning it transcends the social sphere and cannot be reduced to it. The form taken by the court is founded on a desire to apply the law neutrally and objectively and to rationally handle conflicts that, in its absence, would unfold in an arbitrary, unfair, and unequal way, in accordance with power dynamics, domination, and individual interests.

In *Outline of a Phenomenology of Right* Alexandre Kojève insists that the concept of law presupposes that one authority establishes itself in the role of a third party in relation to parties in conflict and to the field of power.[1] The notion of law, of a juridical order, has meaning and validity only if it refers back to an apparatus whose function is to put a stop to and arbitrate wars and individual conflicts. The judicial system thus appears to be an external, specific authority, one not implicated in the private social spheres where it acts as arbitrator.

We can't understand the modern legal apparatus or the judicial sphere without referring back to that claim of impartiality. In a discussion about justice Michel Foucault emphasizes that the ideology of neutrality is visible in and explains the spatial disposition of the courtroom. (Foucault doesn't believe that claim to be warranted, but he nonetheless notes that it allows for an understanding of the court's form and organization.) So, how, in fact, are courtrooms organized? There is "a table, and behind this table, which distances them from the two litigants, the 'third party,' that is, the judges. Their position indicates firstly that they are neutral with respect to each litigant, and secondly this implies that their decision is not already arrived at in advance, that it will be made after an aural investigation of the two parties, on the basis of a certain conception of truth and a certain number of ideas concerning what is just and unjust, and thirdly that they have the authority to enforce their decision."[2]

---

1. See Alexandre Kojève, *Outline of a Phenomenology of Right*, ed. Bryan-Paul Frost, trans. Bryan-Paul Frost and Robert Howse (Lanham, MD: Rowman and Littlefield, 2007).
2. Michel Foucault, "On Popular Justice: A Discussion with Maoists," *Power/Knowledge: Selected Interviews and Other Writings, 1972–1977*, ed. Colin Gordon, trans. Colin Gordon, Leo Marshall, John Mepham, and Kate Soper (New York: Pantheon, 1980), 1–36, 8.

The idea of a power that checks the forces involved and uses universally shared categories or norms of what is "just" and "true," meaning neither specific nor arbitrary, forms the basis of the modern criminal justice system. That portrayal is so powerful that it is even embedded in social geography and urban topography. The centrality and superiority that judicial spaces are meant to incarnate manifest themselves in the way in which, in France for example, courthouses were built and designed until quite recently. The judicial space is conceived of as a "*center that organizes profane space*," writes historian Frédéric Chauvaud in his work on France's criminal courts. French courthouses thus exist as "*separate* spaces within the city, often surrounded by a fence and built *higher* up." Furthermore, "*the door to a courthouse is never located at street level.*"[3]

CRITICAL LEGAL THEORY

The perception of justice as an institution that aims, in its official definition, to incarnate a space of neutrality, independence, and impartiality largely determines the nature of debates on law and criminal justice. It explains—and this is what interests me in particular here—the form taken, since Marx, by critical legal theory, whose near-exclusive objective is to evaluate the extent to which the criminal justice system conforms to its ambitions and claims. This means that the role of critical theory with respect to the state is ambiguous; quite often, it appears to put itself in a reactive position, born from a desire to deconstruct what the state has presented as true. Therein lies the difficulty in imagining what an inventive form of critique could be.

A shared ambition and collective intent can be found among the multitude of discourses arising from critical legal theory:

---

3. Frédéric Chauvaud, *La Chair des prétoires: Histoire sensible de la cour d'assises, 1881–1932* (Rennes: Presses universitaires de Rennes, 2010), 39 (emphasis added).

deconstruction of the values of neutrality, superiority, and universality on which the criminal justice system is supposedly based and the refutation of their applicability. Criticizing the legal-political order consists of resituating justice within a power dynamic, reintegrating the law into conflicts from which it claims to be independent, and recharacterizing the state as an actor and stakeholder in social combats, thereby challenging its role as a fair arbiter.

The task of critique when it comes to the state and juridical order is to reject its founding myths (transcendence, generality, neutrality, and so on) to illustrate its objective participation in the reproduction and legitimization of power dynamics at work in the social world. The law and the courtroom don't represent authorities outside of society and beyond its concerns. On the contrary, they are places where the tactics of domination are deployed and reproduced.

Critical legal theory has thus created a way of characterizing what I have called the "violence" of the law. This approach is principally rooted in the legal system's partiality and particularity and the way in which the universal principles that supposedly undergird it serve, in reality, to foster the perpetuation and legitimization of systems of domination: justice as class justice, an instrument of subjugation, marginalization, exclusion, and discrimination. These terms and concepts constitute the structuring elements of every approach whose object is the law and that defines itself as critique, be it that of Marx, Althusser, or even Bourdieu.

As an illustration of classic legal critique, I'd like to cite an article by Sartre in which he explores the relationship between the state and the law at the moment he is being charged with defamation of the police. What does it mean to him to question the system of judgment? What critical mode does he automatically deploy? His analysis consists of rejecting the characterization of the criminal justice apparatus as a universal and egalitarian institution, designating it instead as a class-based system.

Sartre focuses his attention on the ideological education of judges. He wants to show how any impartiality on their part is impossible:

> The judge is almost always a bourgeois and the son of a bourgeois; his elitist education thus began in childhood. He was put through a competitive course of study, won certain prizes, and emerged a product of this system, a member of the elite by virtue of his ideology, his character, and his profession. Montesquieu wanted accused persons to be judged by their equals in the true sense of the word. This is clearly impossible: because he is the product of a competitive system based on the bourgeois idea that the finest things are the rarest things, the judge feels that he merits his power by his very rarity. He is an important member of the bourgeois hierarchy, and the defendants he judges seem to him to be his inferiors.
>
> Foucault remarks that the topographical analysis of a courtroom—including the bench which separates the judge from the accused person and the witnesses, and the difference in levels between the judge and the others—is enough to indicate that the judge belongs to another species. No matter how impartial he might be, he will treat those who come before him as objects and will make no attempt to understand the subjective motives of their acts as these would appear to the defendants. . . . But these remarks have little to do with the present period. They merely attempt to show what kind of impartiality I expect from a judge. *Let us say that I expect class impartiality, which is a natural wish, since I am going to be appearing before the justice of the bourgeoisie.*[4]

---

4. Jean-Paul Sartre, "Justice and the State," *Life/Situations: Essays Written and Spoken*, trans. P. Auster and L. Davis (New York: Pantheon, 1977), 172–97, This book's translation of the essay is available online at www.oocities.org/c_ansata/JandS.html (emphasis added).

This way of calling the criminal justice system into question reveals that system's dependence on the dominant class's values and ideology and therefore its participation in the perpetuation of domination. This leads to the search for the foundations on which another form of justice—"popular justice"—could be founded, one that would reflect the interests of dominated classes.

Although his vocabulary differs, and his approach is not comparable to that used by Sartre, Foucault adopts the same point of view in his texts on penality, power, and the state. He, too, intends to show how the formal rights and apparatuses of penality are part of the war among different groups; indeed, despite claims to the contrary, they are products of that war much more than they are beyond its reach. In *The Punitive Society* Foucault explicitly states that his approach consists, in contrast to political philosophy, of placing the notion of civil war at the heart of his analysis. A study of penality should use the concept of civil war, of society's internal struggles, as its point of departure. "What has to be brought out first of all in the analysis of a penal system is the nature of the struggles that take place around power in a society."[5]

Foucault's approach echoes and radicalizes the analysis that defines the critique of law: highlight the fact that the law is one of the modes through which social war takes place. As Deleuze writes: "Foucault shows that the law is now no more a state of peace than the result of a successful war: it is war itself, and the strategy of this war in action, just as power is not the property of the dominant class but the strategy of that class in action."[6] Notions of neutrality, impartiality, and shared norms are instruments embedded within a

---

5. Michel Foucault, *The Punitive Society: Lectures at the Collège de France (1972–1973)*, ed. Bernard E. Harcourt, trans. Graham Burchell (London: Palgrave Macmillan, 2015), 13.
6. Gilles Deleuze, *Michel Foucault*, trans. Sean Hand (London: Bloomsbury, 2006), 27–28.

political practice: "All these ideas are weapons which the bourgeoisie has put to use in its exercise of power."[7]

ANOTHER APPROACH

Traditional criticism of the workings of the law seeks to deconstruct the myths of legal normativism and political philosophy. The juridico-political order doesn't function as a body of collective integration and organization. It's an instrument of battle, a weapon, a falsely neutral and falsely transcendent system embedded in political struggles that reproduces social power dynamics. The rhetoric of deconstruction of the law is organized around paired ideas: neutral/violent, impartial/partial, universal/specific, equal/unequal. The actions taken by the justice system are characterized by a radical gap between values of neutrality, impartiality, and equality, and their true impact. This institution therefore masks what it really does, and therein lies its violence. The conflicts within traditional critical theory focus on the modalities of that violence and the nature of social warfare. Recently, the most important debates in this field have concerned the question of whether the law inevitably reproduces inequalities because of its universality or whether, on the contrary, it is the absence of universality, namely, differentiated and discriminatory practices that persist despite formal equality, or the (denied as such) specific nature of legal concepts that should be viewed as responsible.[8]

I understand these criticisms and this analysis perfectly. And I agree that one of the tasks of critical thought is to deconstruct apparatuses that claim to be neutral, impartial, and universal in order to reveal the concrete effects of exclusion, persecution, and

---

7. Foucault, "On Popular Justice," 27.
8. For more on debates in critical theory regarding the law, see Joan W. Scott, *Gender and the Politics of History* (New York: Columbia University Press, 1999), 199–222.

domination they produce. But I also believe that, from this point on, these analyses should be considered givens: they reveal the inequality inherent in abstract liberal law, a fact we don't need to belabor. Critical theory must avoid stagnation, namely by not always repeating the same arguments, however applicable they may be. Progress is possible, and it's vital that we multiply the number of truths revealed and the angles of attack.

I wonder if we should try to go even further in our criticism of the penal state or, more precisely, whether it's possible to proceed differently. Is analyzing neutrality and war enough? Is it possible to go beyond the problems of universality and neutrality, or discrimination and domination when we look at the criminal justice system? In other words, doesn't the organization of debates on this subject obscure another possible critical perspective? Doesn't criticism of "liberal" justice in the name of a "more just" justice (which has at times manifested itself as a call for the establishment of "popular justice" or "class" justice) tend to overlook certain essential foundations of the penal state? We can even ask ourselves if critical legal theory, at times, actually shares certain perceptions with the very legal normativism it's fighting. This would explain why we reencounter—within the idea of "class justice" that Sartre, and others, often used to counter "bourgeois justice" in the 1970s—troubling punitive urges that are strangely similar to those driving the liberal criminal justice machine.

PENALITY AND ACCUSATION

Developing a new critical analysis of the law requires that we modify our view of the legal sphere or, more precisely, that we redirect our gaze on that world, what happens within it, and what matters the most. This therefore entails a change in outlook and focus.

When we think about justice or observe a trial, the figure that immediately attracts our greatest attention is the judge. Of course, I'm not denying that lawyers, defendants, and victims can arouse our interest and curiosity. But the person who seems to best incarnate this institution, its values, and its function is the judge. He appears to be the most important. Sartre focused his attention on judges and their backgrounds when he set out to call his own trial into question. In André Gide's *Recollections of the Assize Court* the presiding judge is omnipresent. Gide makes notes about him on nearly every page, whereas the other figures of the judicial institution are almost completely absent from his account. Raymond Depardon's documentary on one of Paris's district courts, *The 10th District Court: Moments of Trial*, is entirely constructed around the way in which a single judge interacts with defendants.[9]

But that perception leads to ignoring or leaving another essential figure in the shadows, a figure who occupies a decisive position in the judicial process and over the course of a trial: the prosecutor.

Granted, the prosecutor occupies a highly symbolic place in other systems, for example the American or English system. Yet the fact remains that most contemporary legal scholarship conducted within the fields of philosophy, critical theory, or cognitive science focuses on judges' or jurors' decision-making processes, the law and its neutrality, and its varying and discriminatory application, and so forth. When I myself began this project and was considering conducting interviews, I thought it was most important to do so with judges and jurors.

The prosecutor figure is in many ways, in every system, the most unlikable. His discourse is invariably laced with a rare violence, meanness, and aggression toward the accused. Everything, from his statements to his behavior, reflects a desire to punish, reprimand,

---

9. *The 10th District Court: Moments of Trial*, directed by Raymond Depardon (2004; Paris, Arte Éditions, 2005), DVD.

condemn, and exacerbate, even when there is vast uncertainty surrounding proof of guilt.

But, the ways in which he exercises his role notwithstanding, what matters is what this figure represents. It's strange that the prosecutor has such a minimal presence, in comparison to the judge, in discourses critical of the legal system. This is primarily because he implies the existence of an extremely strong ideological and political machine. This figure says something about the way in which the state takes hold of individuals, the workings of the law and the logic of punishment, and what it means to be a subject of the law.

In effect, during a trial, the prosecutor represents the "state." He defends "the interests of society." He supports the prosecution. Put another way, it suffices to attend a trial to realize that the vision of justice as an arbiter between two parties, which has nonetheless dramatically shaped thinking about the institution, is false. This is because—and this is equally true of the French, US, and British systems—the criminal trial does not pit a defendant against a victim who comes before a judge or judges to register a complaint or accusation. Instead, the system of judgment creates an arena in which an individual appears before what we call "society," which is defended by its lawyer, which is to say, the prosecutor. The repressive state apparatus rests on the idea that when I act, I don't only, or perhaps even primarily, harm the individual(s) I directly injure: first and foremost, I wrong "society." As a result, the state can pursue proceedings against me according to a procedure that unfolds with relative autonomy in relation to civil procedure or even in the absence of a civil procedure and an individual victim: criminal procedure. This type of criminal justice apparatus, a system in which charges are brought by a prosecutor, exists in nearly every state governed by the rule of law in the world, or at least in the French, American, and British systems, meaning that the analysis I propose here applies to each.

In the United States the prosecutor is the lawyer of "the People," and a criminal trial pits the people of a state against the accused, for example, "the People of the State of New York" versus "X."

Focusing on the political construction of the actions within the logic of the criminal justice system provides a very powerful way not only to understand justice but also to grasp the power operations applied to us by the state through modern law. It's not so much the act of judging as the act of accusing that interests me here: To what must we be answerable? What are we accused of? By whom? What am I being reproached for when I am reproached for something under criminal law? What do I "do" when I do something? In short, this approach doesn't seek to determine how I am "judged" nor whether or not I am "guilty" but to reflect on the state's construction of the crime of which I'm accused, on my actions and their meanings.

These questions pave the way for a broader reflection on sovereignty, the logic of repression, the violence of the law, and political use of the legal system—and even more profoundly, in my opinion, on the lingering antidemocratic aspects of the contemporary form of the rule of law.

THE LOGIC OF PUNISHMENT

TRAUMA AND REACTIONS TO TRAUMA

When exploring questions of crime, law, and penality, we are inevitably confronted by the issue of trauma and of reactions to the aggression experienced. A psychic economy of injury pushes us to respond to violence with violence and to transform the shock of trauma into an act of force directed against the other (or others) intended to cause suffering.

In *On the Genealogy of Morality* Nietzsche describes the way in which the institution of justice is linked to and stems from the logic of trauma and compensation: enduring trauma engenders an inclination to want to cause suffering. The psychic need to complete that cycle of reactions drives us to punish and reprimand and, therefore, to seek out the responsible party. In other words, justice doesn't rely, initially, on the establishment of a logic of responsibility. It reflects an economy of injuries. At the origin of criminal law we can observe the belief that it is possible to find an equivalency between injury and pain: the injury endured seems to necessitate, as fair compensation, the administration of pain to another party. And it matters little if, ultimately, that third party is the true author of the injury inflicted or whether he or she voluntarily caused it or not. The injury demands that someone be punished, and this requirement lies at the foundation of the construction of criminal law and justice. We don't want to punish someone because he or she is seen as being responsible. Rather, we designate someone as responsible because we want to punish and inflict suffering: "For the longest period of human history punishment was definitely *not* meted out *because* the perpetrator was held responsible for his deed, therefore *not* under the presupposition that only the guilty one was to be punished:—rather, just as parents today still punish their children, from anger over injury suffered."[1]

I am personally convinced of the vast power of the psychic economy described by Nietzsche, which can be found at the root of the dynamics of repression and punishment. Any critique of the criminal justice system and the repressive apparatus must therefore explore the relationship between these apparatuses and that psychic drive. Ultimately, a legal system has meaning and relevance only if it represents a rationalizing instrument that filters spontaneous perceptions and if it functions as a technique of subjectification that allows, or even forces, us to step back from ourselves and our initial impulses in order to pacify the world. Formulating a critique of repression and repressive drives consists in asking ourselves to what extent the modern system of penality establishes a more rational—or even, as we will see, more democratic—order in comparison to spontaneous logics of passion or if it endorses these logics and makes room for them in the rule of law.

From this point of view it's impossible not to wonder whether there's something odd and, indeed, paradoxical about the criminal

---

1. Friedrich Nietzsche, *Beyond Good and Evil / On the Genealogy of Morality*, trans. Adrian Del Caro, vol. 8 of *The Complete Works of Friedrich Nietzsche* (Stanford, CA: Stanford University Press, 2014), 252.

justice system in which we evolve and which has such sway over us. The prosecutor who replaces the victim during a trial unquestionably represents, in a sense, an important institution and is even a mark of progress. This figure is part of a framework intended to manage reactions to crime in a rational and dispassionate way as compared to the spontaneous reactions of victims or their loved ones. A filter is established between judicial logic and the passionate logic of trauma and reactions to injury. This is often especially important in cases of self-defense, where the prosecution can choose not to relay plaintiffs' demands for sanctions by citing legal or rational imperatives.

But strangely enough, the criminal justice apparatus seems to break with spontaneous emotional reactions only to proceed itself with a phantasmatic treatment of illegal activity that reflects a desire for punishment that is hard to justify from a rational perspective. What, then, does penal logic signify? It means that, when a crime occurs, the state dispossesses the victim of what has happened and takes his or her place; the state positions itself as the victim—and even, more precisely, as the primary victim. In short: it adds another crime to the one committed. It adds a victim. It creates two violent acts from one: the first occurs in the civil domain and the second, in parallel, in the penal one. The penal state creates two crimes where only one existed: one committed against the victim, the other against the state.

How can we understand this practice through which the state constructs two crimes out of one? Does framing a crime as a crime against the public order and designating every criminal act as an assault against "society" actually establish a rational order? Or does it in fact reproduce a cycle of violence that uses us in order to function? Isn't this equivalent to responding to violence with violence and to trauma with trauma? And can't this apparatus consequently inflict violence and trauma on victims themselves by placing them in a situation of helplessness and dispossession? I'm not criticizing the law as such. There are different conceptions of law and justice, not all of which are constructed in this way. I'm questioning penal logic and the system of punishment to evaluate whether these institutions are faithful to their potential emancipatory usage—or if, on the contrary, they are governed by questionable logics whose nature we should evaluate, whose effects we should understand, and whose aims we should determine. Does the law in fact administer justice?

THE LOGIC OF PENALITY

In *The Division of Labor in Society* Emile Durkheim proposes an analysis whose principles can be used to reflect on the logic of criminal law, the operations present in the construction of the law, and what that can tell us about the state and the powers it applies to us through the system of punishment.

Durkheim distinguishes between two types of law: repressive and restitutive.[2] Repressive law is criminal (or penal) law: it has an expiatory function; it inflicts suffering on the guilty party through an organized system of sanctions: a reduction in one's fortune, honor, or freedom. It aims to deprive the individual of something. Restitutive law is mainly incarnated by civil law: its goal is to provide reparations for wrongs. Civil justice settles for organizing interindividual reparation for injuries caused by the criminal act in order to restore the initial situation, whereas criminal justice *adds something*: it reprimands the act *and* punishes the actor. We are therefore dealing with two systems and two conceptions that are completely different and autonomous and that at times coexist (civil proceedings can occur in parallel with criminal proceedings

---

2. See Emile Durkheim, *The Division of Labor in Society*, trans. Lewis A. Coser (New York: Free Press, 1997).

for similar crimes) and at other times are completely disconnected (a criminal proceeding can take place without a civil one). The privileged instrument of criminal sanctions in contemporary societies is the deprivation of freedom; the instruments of civil reparation are damages and interests.

Durkheim shows that the type of law, and consequently reactions to crime, dominant in each society varies according to the era: these laws depend on how a society is structured and the meaning it attributes to the criminal act. In closely knit societies or groups where the collective consciousness has a strong hold and the division of labor is weak, every crime is perceived as a crime against all—one that affects each individual as a member of society. The crime threatens social cohesion by disrupting universally recognized rules. It therefore prompts a societal reaction intended to maintain social cohesion and the collective consciousness. Compensation between parties isn't enough. The society as a whole also wants to express its dissatisfaction and right a wrong. Punishment is necessary: a penal, repressive, and expiatory sanction. Criminal law reflects a social state in which crime is experienced and perceived (meaning constructed) as a threat to society.

Conversely, the logic of restitution dominates when social solidarity has been affected by processes of labor division and individualization, that is, when the hold of the collective consciousness on its agents has weakened. A more complex society, in which individuals are more differentiated and less alike, looks less like an integrated space in which everyone feels affected by what happens to others than like a system in which more or less connected diverse and partial sectors coexist. Restitutive law, then, applies to the majority of acts, whose reach is perceived as local. Individual actions don't concern "society" as a whole, only specific and restricted parts. In this context the consequences of transgressions are handled at the local, not global, level. Wrongs are repaired, and punishment does not appear necessary.

Durkheim's objective is fundamentally sociological and historical. He formulates a law of the evolution of criminal justice: the individualization and differentiation of societies goes hand in hand with a transformation of the way that they construct crimes and criminal acts and envisage reactions to illegal activity. The historical shift has been toward relatively strengthened civil law in comparison to criminal law: decentralized compensation has increased to the detriment of collective punishment because the more divided and heterogeneous a society is, the more events that occur within it are experienced as having only local and partial consequences. This, of course, doesn't mean that criminal law has disappeared. It remains quite present in modern societies. Nonetheless, according to Durkheim, the trend has been to decriminalize numerous acts while maintaining criminal law for the most serious offenses, which continue to offend and shock what Durkheim calls the "collective consciousness."

As is often the case with sociology, Durkheim's study becomes more interesting and valuable when it is used for critical and political purposes. We should convert and transpose Durkheim's analyses from a historical context to a conceptual one. What, then, does Durkheim's analysis reveal? Namely the fact that approaches to crime and responses to illegal activity are in no way spontaneous or natural. They are institutions or, to use critical vocabulary, power apparatuses, susceptible to transformation. In other words, justice is always based on a symbolic and narrative construction, which opens it up to historicity and discussion. Criminal law and restitutive law are practices of power. They concretize different ways of reacting to the trauma of an aggression, organizing the system of punishment and violence, and constructing what is at stake in a given crime and what it impacts.

Durkheim's analysis gives us the instruments to conduct a critical investigation of both ourselves and the logic of penality and punishment. It reveals the cryptic aspect of the presence of a figure like the prosecutor at a trial. It invites us to reflect on and take a step back from the strange practice of adding a logic of punishment to the logic of compensation—meaning the fact that a delinquent is sanctioned both for his or her act against another person and for the supposed act against "society." Why should I, when I steal something, in addition to paying reparation to my "victim," have to pay something to the state and spend time in prison? What is the purpose of this ritual aspect of sanctions? What is the real damage done to the state? Why add punishment on top of punishment? Understanding the juridical order under which we live thus demands that we think about the concepts, mechanisms, and constructions that undergird the logic of penality—and, on that basis, grasp the power effects exerted by that juridical practice and the political reasoning in which it is embedded.

TRANSFIGURATION

In the history of the theory and practice of criminal justice there are essentially two major ways of justifying and promoting the logic of punishment. The first consists of affirming that any singular act is an aggression against "society" or "the nation." This is why, when I injure someone or steal from someone, "reparations" aren't enough—I've affected everyone. I've "disturbed the public order." I must therefore be held accountable for that aggression to the other victim of my act—the state or society. Cesare Beccaria explains this concept in *On Crimes and Punishments*, a seminal work of modern penality: "Every crime, even of the most private nature, injures society," and as a result, the only true measure of a crime is "by the injury done to society."[3] Dozens of similar conclusions can be found in existing scholarship, notably Durkheim's famous descriptions of crime as an act that offends the collective consciousness and criminal law as an institution designed to protect social cohesion from deviant forces that aim to weaken it. According to Durkheim, there are two kinds of acts that criminal law "prohibits and labels as crimes": "Either they directly manifest too much of a violent contrast between the characteristics of the offender and those of the collective type, or else they offend against the organ of the common consciousness. In both cases the force that is offended by the crime and suppresses it is the same. It is a product of the most vital social similarities, and it has the result of maintaining the social cohesion that derives from these similarities. It is this force that penal law protects against being undermined."[4]

Clearly, from a critical viewpoint we can't consider Beccaria's or Durkheim's declarations to be constative statements. They are, on the contrary, performative acts that benefit the apparatuses of power. Both make the logic of modern penality possible and conceivable, activating and reinforcing it. Durkheim's definition that an "act is criminal when it offends the strong, well-defined states of the collective consciousness," which explains why it "require[s] from us a higher sanction than the mere reparation,"[5] should be substituted with the idea that the very notion of a "collective consciousness" is a rhetorical strategy used to legitimize practices of power and repression.

Criminal justice rests on the performative construction of crime as a social act. It is predicated on a process that transfigures every

---

3. Cesare Beccaria, *On Crimes and Punishment*, trans. Edward D. Ingraham (N.p.: Seven Treasures Publications, 2009), 19, 26.
4. Kenneth Thompson, ed., *Readings from Emile Durkheim* (London: Routledge, 2005), 22.
5. Durkheim, *The Division of Labor in Society*, 39, 56.

individual act into one that affects that abstract reality we call "society" rather than an act against other individuals that takes place on the horizontal plane of social interactions. Modern justice is a system in which interindividual actions are reshaped by the state into actions against "society."

There is an incredibly strong link between the repressive state apparatus as a system of power and essentialist notions like "nation" and "society." The vision of individual actions shaped by those concepts suits and benefits the criminal justice machine. In many ways those notions establish and legitimize it. They make it possible to imagine that a "crime" goes beyond the victim/aggressor pairing, to something broader beyond that horizontal plane, and that it therefore necessitates a separate reaction that must take the form of expiation and repression. A radical critique of penality and repressive urges must therefore question substantialist categories (nation, public order, society) and their legal and political use.

ABSTRACTION

The logic of penality and the dynamics of punishment are not based solely on a construction of acts as affecting "society." Or perhaps I should say that the state's justification of its repressive interference doesn't rely solely on socializing arguments. Political philosophy is yet another major domain that produces representations that give rise to and support the idea of criminal law.

Rousseau's *Social Contract* offers an example of a text in which we can see a theoretical and symbolic logic at work—a vision of the world that makes the penal apparatus possible. It employs a group of discursive and rhetorical operations aimed at justifying the criminal justice system, which shows to what extent the latter relies on symbolic foundations that are far from obvious or self-explanatory and that we are wrong to consider as such. Rousseau constructs crime as much more than, and even completely different from, an aggression by one individual against another. That said, he doesn't frame the crime as an attack against "society" but as the moment when the "criminal" directly confronts the "general will."

Society becomes a political institution, a body, through the establishment of law. Being a member of a political community, a citizen, means adopting the general will as one's own and recognizing one's own adhesion to that community's laws. Consequently, breaking the law amounts to demonstrating one's "foreignness" or exteriority to the law and, therefore, to the political community. One becomes a dissident subject in relation to the general will by breaking its hold and weakening it. As a result, a crime is not a private matter; it's a political one. Transgressions undermine the law and the general will and threaten the cohesion of the entire political body.

Being a criminal, disobeying the law, means manifesting a will that differs from the general will, which simultaneously represents the citizen's will and ensures the unity of the body politic. Through his act the criminal denies that he is a citizen and excludes himself from the political community: "Every malefactor, by attacking social rights, becomes on forfeit a rebel and a traitor to his country; by violating its laws he ceases to be a member of it; he even makes war upon it. In such a case the preservation of the State is inconsistent with his own, and one or the other must perish; in putting the guilty to death, we slay not so much the citizen as an enemy. The trial and the judgment are the proofs that he has broken the social treaty, and is in consequence no longer a member of the State."[6]

Strikingly, this same rhetoric and vision also appears in Kant's "The Doctrine of Right." Like Rousseau, Kant views crime as a transgression against the state and therefore the criminal as a traitor

---

6. Jean-Jacques Rousseau, *The Social Contract* (New York: Hafner, 1947), 31.

and public enemy. For him, "transgression of a public law" renders the criminal "unfit to be a citizen."[7]

Kant's text is entirely devoted to praise for the criminal justice system, which takes in the form of a radical critique of reparative conceptions of justice or utilitarian ideas of punishment. The role of punishment is never simply to repair the damages inflicted on an individual or individuals. When a crime is committed, reparation alone doesn't suffice. Something more is needed (criminal repression always represents that *something more*): atonement and punishment—in other words penalization: "*Punishment by a court . . . can never be inflicted merely as a means to promote some other good for the criminal himself or for civil society. It must always be inflicted upon him only because he has committed a crime.*"[8]

Kant's position opposes any application of a utilitarian argument for justice. He considers it inconceivable to approach the question of punishment in terms of costs and benefits, interest, or social utility. The punishment of a crime should be unconditional, regardless of its utility and potential costs. He takes theft as an example of a crime that must be punished beyond any damage caused to the victim. Merely compensating the victim isn't enough. Why not? Because it's society as a whole that must make the criminal atone, for he or she, by committing a crime, has destabilized the judicial structures supporting the social and political order: "Whoever steals anything makes the property of all insecure." In this sense the transgressor ruins the system of property as a whole and weakens "*all security in property.*"[9]

The justification of penality is predicated on framing transgression of the law as an autonomous problem in and of itself. The

---

7. Immanuel Kant, *The Metaphysics of Morals*, rev. ed., ed. Lara Denis, trans. Mary Gregor (Cambridge: Cambridge University Press, 2017), 114.
8. Ibid., 114.
9. Ibid.

law incarnates the public order and the will of the state; respect for the law shows recognition of the state, its authority, and its legitimacy. The transgression, then, constitutes an act of disobedience and dissent, which merits punishment *independent of all other possible considerations*. The question of material and real damages becomes entirely irrelevant. The institution of criminal law assumes that each crime be constructed as a challenge to something, to an entity—the public order, society, the state—that is situated beyond the immanent scope of social and interpersonal life. Consequently, justice must punish the offense, which is irreducible to the injury inflicted on the victim, through the state's appropriation of the guilty party's property (a fine) and punishment (prison).

Texts by Rousseau, Kant, and even Durkheim show the extent to which the conception of action and its effects on which the state punitive apparatus rests, or that is invoked by the state punitive apparatus as its foundation, is anything but self-evident or natural. It's an artifice, a construction, and finally a political technique.

Penality conveys a kind of state takeover of our lives: what happens to us seems to happen simultaneously to the state, ensuring that the state feels legitimized when it reacts in its own interest and as if it were, in fact, the primary victim.

The idea of punishment implies a transmutation of actions, in which the acts through which individuals harm one another are converted into acts that harm all of society—whether this last is designated by the "general will," "*res publica*," or "collective consciousness." There is a connection between the logic of punishment and the logic of the state's dispossession of us and our actions.

The penal state also applies a process of abstraction and universalization to each crime, thereby situating it within a more general dynamic of defiance of the law. This is why, during a trial, a robbery is never, ultimately, judged as *a* robbery. Instead, the question rapidly shifts to *robbery in general*, to *theft in general*, and, consequently, to security and the fundamental right to property—as if a localized act had affected and weakened the entirety of judicial structures and the legal edifice.

The tradition stretching from Rousseau to Hegel, and including Kant, that seeks to justify the logic of penality thus tends to invent a kind of dramatic (I might even say unbelievable) scenario in which every crime, even the smallest or most specific, is ultimately presented and taken as a critical moment during which the very possibility of the law, the authority of the general will, and the cohesion of the political order are at stake. No wonder, then, that these authors grant punishment an essential role and accentuate its severity. From this perspective its function consists of nothing less than, on every occasion, restoring and maintaining the social order, sovereign power, and authority of the political body: the justification of power and the fueling of the powers that be—what a strange conception of the role of the intellectual!

WHAT IS A CRIME?
THE FICTIONAL FRAMEWORKS OF PENALITY

A judicial system is characterized by the way in which it collectively deploys two distinct apparatuses that are relatively independent from one another but that are nonetheless rarely analyzed as such in critical scholarship: a system of judgment, on one hand, and a system of punishment, on the other. These two different systems each obey their own logic—ensuring that the penal state is a complex institution that cannot be reduced to a binary vision.

First, the system of judgment establishes a certain way of explaining what happens in the world, of understanding actors' behavior and the causes of their actions: Who is responsible? Who did this? For what reasons? And how to explain it? Then the system of repression intervenes: it organizes the *reaction to the action* and the determination of the sanction according to how the infraction and its consequences are perceived.

The modern penal state operates paradoxically. As we saw in the previous section, the system of judgment applied to us is characterized by a fundamentally antisociological dimension: justice constructs an individualizing narrative of the causes of actions; it desocializes and dehistoricizes actors; and it refuses to take social determinants into account. Yet, oddly enough, the system of punishment is linked to social concepts. The state uses categories ("society," "nation," "public order") that socialize actions *in terms of their consequences* and thus establishes the perception that particular behaviors always and inevitably disrupt *something else*: "all of society," the "public order," or the "entire nation."

Contrary to what they claim, these discursive operations don't express a reality. Their observations are not true. Rather, they create fictions intended to subjugate and that must therefore be deconstructed by sociology. Used in this way, notions like "society," "nation," or "public order" represent abstract, meaningless concepts that phantasmatically overdetermine the meaning of acts in order to legitimize the exercise of effects of power. We thus find ourselves dealing with what we could label an antisociological use of socializing concepts. Having desocializing actors, the penal state "socializes" actions, as if it wanted to render each of us potentially responsible for even more than what we have really done in order to strengthen its hold over us.

It's impossible to understand what is going on during a trial by concentrating on the judgment passed or the application—be it neutral or case-by-case—of the law. Something else, something subtler, is at work: the construction of what is actually being judged, the criminal matter itself. A trial's first objective is to justify itself and the penal construction of reality. Every criminal trial, including for misdemeanors for that matter, represents a moment of transfiguration. Actions are redefined as behaviors that supposedly affect a larger body, ensuring that the conclusions we're meant to draw fall obligatorily under the umbrella of punitive justice and slip away from the actors themselves, meaning all that is civil, compensatory, and restitutive. A trial's implicit function is to legitimize the logic of criminal sanctions and sharpen repressive urges.

Grasping this objective allows us to become aware of the central role of the prosecutor figure, to the detriment of that of the judge. The former represents "society" and the "public order"; he incarnates the logic of the criminal justice system. His actions and statements therefore play a crucial role. They aren't meant, as we might believe, to "prove" the defendant's "guilt" (which, in most of the cases I observed, was hardly in doubt) but to *construct acts and their meaning*. They attempt to give new meaning to the question "What am I guilty of?" or "What did I do?" During a trial, everything indicates that its most important element consists of publicly telling defendants, You did more than you think. Your actions are more serious than you believe. You didn't just steal/assault/etc.; you endangered all of society, weakened the order of law, and defied the state.

I'd like to reflect on the violent operations of that overdetermination and their political and psychological consequences using the examples of two criminal trials I observed. The two trials were very different and the two cases incomparable. But in both we can see an operation of increasing generality that inscribes the act being judged within a series of autonomous meanings to which it does not belong. Using these examples, I'd like to identify the rhetorical techniques, abstract categories, and socializing arguments that support the punitive action: What methods does the state use to reconstruct reality and dramatize the stakes? How does it impose a series of autonomous meanings on a given act in order to tell the defendant, You must be punished and you will be punished severely? And how should a critique of punishment lead us to construct other languages and other ways in which to relate to and construct reality?

TERRORISM

The first case was tried in September of 2011 in Paris's assizes court and dealt with an attempted bombing in connection with a terrorist organization—Corsican nationalists. Two young men were accused of involvement in this attempt: three explosive devices were placed in front of a group of empty secondary residences one night; none of them worked. When the group that had placed the devices realized that they hadn't exploded as scheduled, the two defendants were asked to go verify what had happened and, if needed, to retrigger them.

What interests me here is not the question of the defendants' guilt but rather understanding how the trial, from start to finish, consisted of constructing a representation of these three explosive devices and the acts being judged. It was striking to see how, from the indictment order to the prosecution's closing speech, politics and history were used to dramatize, by overdetermination, the actions the court had to address and understand.

The charges, read by the court clerk at the trial's start, began—and this struck me as very strange—by narrating the evolution of the Corsican nationalist movement since the beginning of the 2000s. This included mention of a multitude of actions *attributed* to that movement: shootings at police stations or government buildings, assassinations, score settling, trafficking, bombings, various disturbances. In other words, the trial didn't begin with the actual facts of the case. It used history—the narration of a succession of events categorized as Corsican nationalism—and politics—the idea of a "separatist," "terrorist" movement that challenges the state's authority with its every act—in order to establish a transcendent framework in relation to which the truth would be determined. Here, then, was a confrontation between the state's authority and Corsican nationalism, a confrontation itself regarded as a specific case of terrorism and the struggle against it. The meaning behind the acts being judged was to be reconstructed and determined in relation to that sociopolitical reality.

The phantasmatic logic undergirding the criminal justice system appeared in all its breadth—and violence—when the prosecutor delivered her closing argument, revealing the extent to which abstract concepts are tightly linked to drives for order and punishment. The prosecutor employed rhetoric that framed the acts being judged as signifiers of terrorism in general. As a result, she could say to the judges, Your decision and the sentences you hand down constitute participation in the war that states must wage against terrorism. The violence of criminal punishment in this case thus stemmed from the symbolic construction of three small devices as apparatuses that incarnated the contemporary dangers weighing on democratic societies.

The prosecutor began her closing argument by going back to the 1970s: she spoke about the history of the nationalist movement; she emphasized the "ten thousand" bombings carried out in Corsica over the past "thirty years"; she dramatized; she mentioned the "cowardly assassination of the prefect Claude Érignac." She shouted: "All this must stop!"

The defendants, whom she admitted were not "big fish"—that is, important figures within the movement—were treated similarly. According to the prosecutor, they "belonged to the organization." From that perspective, even if they were only charged with complicity, they were no different from "those who acted." They represented the organization as a whole.

This case is extremely instructive. Ultimately, the devices didn't explode. In other words, no injury was caused, and for that matter no one pursued a civil action. From that point on, the prosecutor and more broadly the trial had one very specific and strange function: *to create injury and invent entities that were harmed* by those three small devices—society, the public order, democracy, "our security." Those devices, which caused no material or physical damage (meaning no damage at all), and the two young defendants on the fringes of a nationalist movement came to incarnate the threats weighing on the security of us all ("when you place a bomb, you never know what will happen"), the freedom of citizens, and the functioning of democracy.

The dramatization of judged acts constitutes an apparatus essential to the logic of punishment. Historical or political concepts are never used to explain or understand defendants and their trajectories but as instruments to create out of whole cloth both acts and their supposed impact: the destabilization of the state. Hence, a punishment incommensurate with the damage objectively caused (in this case, nonexistent) but in accordance with the imaginary damage invented by society, through the prosecutor's speech, to satisfy a repressive logic. One of the defendants was sentenced to five years' imprisonment, the other to eight.

PSYCHOLOGY AND SOCIETY

The second example I will analyze is a case of rape and illegal confinement: a man was accused of locking a woman in his bedroom and raping her several times in the course of one night. In a way, one can imagine that the injury inflicted on the victim, meaning the act in its singularity, would be sufficient to determine and justify the punishment. Yet strikingly, once again, the judicial process in this case attributed new meaning to the crime in question. A rape is not only a specific act in which one person assaults another. It's more than that. The particular rape addressed by the court became a singular expression of general tendencies that disrupt society as a whole. It was essentially on behalf of that *social component* that the rape in question would be judged and punished.

In cases of terrorism, history and politics are invoked to produce a generalization of the criminal act and to integrate it within a much larger ensemble that amplifies its significance. Here, it was a psychiatric and psychological construction of the crime that was decisive.

Of course, as I showed earlier, psychiatry and psychology are embedded within the apparatus of individualization: they serve to endogenize social forces and codify our relationship to the world in the form of a relationship to self. But their complicity with the penal state doesn't end there. They play a supplementary role that doesn't appear in the explanations that they provide for crimes but in their description of the relationships between the offender, his acts, and the world around him. Expert testimonies support the logic of punishment by creating an image of the crime and the criminal as a concrete menace that threatens all of society.

In this case of rape and unlawful confinement a psychologist and a psychiatrist presented their expert opinions to the court and jury.

The psychologist spoke first. She began by describing her examination of the defendant who, she noted, was afraid that "his words would be twisted": he refused to talk about his background and personality. The defendant justified this attitude by maintaining that he was "distrustful" and that, furthermore, talking about his childhood and history made him "want to cry." But the expert drew conclusions about the accused's personality based on this refusal to meet her demands. This refusal revealed the defendant's "low self-esteem." He also demonstrated that he had a "low tolerance for frustration": given that the tests (I believe they were Rorschach tests) were long, a little tedious, and demanded some effort, the defendant had refused to take them.

Once she had made her two diagnoses—"low self-esteem" and "low tolerance for frustration"—naturally, without ever mentioning immigration, racism, the defendant's relationship to school or language (he was dyslexic), economic hardships, previous run-ins with the government, etc.—the psychologist really laid into her subject. She assembled a series of qualifiers to describe the defendant: distrustful, compulsive, anxious, lacking a parental role model, extremely fragile, ill-equipped, impoverished sex life, no sexual relations with anyone his own age, and so on.

This kind of apocalyptic description isn't gratuitous. Above all, within the apparatus of the trial it is anything but neutral. In this case it allowed the psychologist to present the rape as the manifestation of a structurally disturbed relationship to the world and against which the world as a whole should defend itself. For that matter, the presiding judge used this moment to ask the expert: "Is he capable of having nonviolent interactions with women?" The psychologist answered: "He admits to great difficulty approaching others. He finds interactions with women extremely anxiety provoking due to his fear of rejection. And therefore, approaching a woman with the goal of a relationship between consenting adults is inordinately distressing to him."

A few hours later, the psychiatrist testified. His name is Roland Coutanceau, and he is rather well known in France. His testimony was difficult to watch. It was clear that he enjoyed being there and using the symbolic power provided by his position as an expert. Furthermore, it was impossible not to be bothered by the rather summary way he established himself as an authoritative scientist (he kept repeating "I'll say this in my jargon, then I'll explain," or "I'm using scientific language here, but I'll translate afterwards") in order to ensure that his statements impressed the jurors. Incidentally, there is generally something unpleasant about psychiatrists' attitudes when they address the court: they use their "symbolic authority" almost consciously, as well as what they believe to be their "expertise," to do violence to the accused, intensify the punishment, and recommend still greater sanctions and severity. They never seem to have a guilty conscience, nor do they seem driven by a minimum of ethical concern for maintaining distance from the exercise of power. Contrary to what we might fairly expect from individuals presenting themselves as "intellectuals" or "scientists," they submit to the repressive state apparatus and place themselves at its service.

Coutanceau also described his examination of the defendant, mentioning the intellectual level and background of the accused. Then the expert came to the phase that interested him: the diagnosis of the defendant's "personality"—meaning his "defining traits." He insisted, of course, on the existence of a "personality disorder," characterized by three main elements: "fundamental immaturity," "paranoid tendencies," and, finally, "egocentric volubility." He added that the subject was affected by the "absence of parental frames of reference," resulting in an instinctive, impulsive, and infantile individual who responded to a "need-based sexuality."

The accused was also supposedly a conflicted individual, who behaved, according to the psychiatrist, like a "chameleon." On the one hand, explained the "expert," using an image he judged simple enough for the jurors, the defendant resembled "Belmondo in certain films": extroverted, at ease, flirtatious—his immature side. But, internally, his paranoia made him closed-off, rigid, distrustful, and depressed; he expressed a feeling of persecution that constituted, according to the psychiatrist, a strategy typically used by paranoiacs to justify their aggression ("I felt like I was being mistreated, so I responded with violence"). This mix of volubility, immaturity, and paranoia maintained a cycle of violence that had never been nor could be controlled, ensuring that unless punished, and provided with subsequent medical care, the defendant would present a "proven dangerousness."

During this case of rape and unlawful confinement the psychiatrist and psychologist painted what they called a clinical portrait of the defendant's personality. Although these linguistic elements may appear secondary or anecdotal, in reality they occupy a critical position within the trial apparatus. They support and accentuate the logic of punishment. In this case the described traits would be repeated by the prosecutor during her closing argument. Following a typical sequence, she constructed the individual on trial as a deviant figure who exists "outside of his crime," to borrow Foucault's expression. She depicted him using the traits of a "sexual predator" who displayed an "extreme criminological dangerousness."

What was the point of the trial? What happened during the three days of proceedings? It wasn't really a question of guilt and responsibility. Instead, the defendant's past, his personality assessments, and his criminal record, as well as medical and psychological expertise, gradually accumulated to transform a specific rape into a more general behavior. In other words, psychiatric discourse doesn't merely serve to individualize a given act. Yes, it isolates the author of said act from the world by presenting the cause of his actions as the expression of an internal dynamic. But, at the same time, this discourse socializes acts and their consequences: it depicts the crime as a threat weighing on everybody. In this sense, any offense is considered an aggression against "society."

Remember that, according to Rousseau, every crime constitutes a war between a deviant individual and society. The consequences of the psychiatric perspective are not far removed from that notion. A crime is presented as the tip of the iceberg and the moment in which a structural asociality that threatens and harms society is actualized. The criminal's existence constitutes an aggression that concerns everyone. It disrupts social life. So here again, we find an implicit representation—the criminal at war with society—that forms the basis of the idea that society should wage war against him. Legal logic, abstract logic, and psychiatric logic constitute three essential foundations for the logic of punishment. Psychiatric discourse thus manages to support and benefit the penal state both in terms of the system of judgment and the system of punishment.

In her book *La Vie ordinaire des assises* (The everyday life of the court), Marie-Pierre Courtellemont describes eight trials she observed; she also recreates the inclusive logic and techniques of dramatization that structure the logic behind the criminal justice system and are at the heart of the prosecutor's statements. Courtellemont mentions, for example, a trial for armed robbery held at the assizes court of Versailles, which, thanks to the prosecutor, became a trial for armed robbery and theft in general: "Ladies and gentlemen, as you deliberate, I'd like to ask you to close your eyes for two minutes and imagine. Imagine the screams, the violence. Except that we're not at the movies. This isn't make-believe. There were *six hundred armed robberies* in Yvelines over the past two months. *That's a lot. Do not trivialize armed robberies.*"[1] Further on in the book, the author describes another case: a trial for the rape of minors, in which the victims' father and a family friend were the defendants. Here again, the prosecutor's case was built by describing the offenses in question as specific examples of a collective threat. He characterized them as part of a global phenomenon, and the trial was presented as a critical moment in the societal reaction to the weakening of the incest taboo, which imperils childhood: "I am charged with ensuring social peace, with making sure private justice is avoided. But society cannot exist unless incest is forbidden [prosecutors make these kind of statements, which they appear to find very intelligent, all the time]. Children deserve protection because they are fragile, because they are still being formed. *Child rape now represents one case in two judged before the criminal court in our department, Seine-Saint-Denis.*

---

1. Marie-Pierre Courtellemont, *La Vie ordinaire des assises* (Paris: Ramsay, 2005), 205.

These children are paying for their parents' sins. This is a collective danger. So, are the defendants guilty? I think so."²

CONCLUSION

Three devices are framed as entities that put democracy at risk: a rape is treated as the actualization of an aggressiveness that threatens the social order; a robbery is transformed into a symbol of insecurity; the rape of a child weakens the incest taboo and represents a collective threat. These kinds of rhetorical moves illustrate the way in which the logic of punishment depends on a practice of overdetermination. In criminal law a crime is never, in the end, judged for what it truly is. The act is systematically constructed as affecting a global reality performatively constructed by the law and during the course of a trial.

We could even say that, in a sense, the accused are always, in one way or another, punished for acts that they didn't commit—the nature and meaning of those acts having been created by the state *after the fact and during the trial*. We can almost dare to say that we are always punished for something that we didn't do. The idea of punishment presupposes that acts are given new meaning by the judicial institution, which transforms them in relation to the reality of their embeddedness in local situations and specific contexts. The violence of criminal justice stems, in large part, from this practice of overdetermination. Indeed, the practice allows acts to be punished in a way that is incommensurate with the objective damages caused and is, in fact, fairly proportional to the violence that the criminal justice system itself has designated and attributed to them.³

---

2. Ibid., 309.
3. In *La Justice en procès* (Paris: Presses de Sciences-Po, 2013) Jean Bérard assembles, in quite an interesting way, feminist traditions that criticize how the criminal justice system treats rape and the way in which prosecutors and judges appropriate this issue.

All of this means that the popular distinction, so often made in judicial theory, between common law crimes and political crimes appears vaguer and more uncertain than ever. The very notion of penality presupposes that every crime or infraction, however ordinary, commonplace, or specific, be framed and then judged as a crime or offense against society or the state—and therefore as a political crime. And the logic behind the sanction itself, which has the state instituting a specific punishment for that assault against the "social body" and challenge to the rule of law, can only be understood as representing a political ritual through which sovereign power publicly reestablishes its authority and seeks to erase the affront that's been done to it, *according to it*, in order to affirm itself as the state.

PENALITY, SOVEREIGNTY, AND DEMOCRACY

The question that necessarily arises in every critique of the system of punishment is that of knowing on what basis, and how, to challenge the criminal justice apparatus. It's hard to imagine something different, to visualize what another, less repressive and less violent, form of law could be. That is also why it's so difficult to grasp what is truly problematic about the system we know and what might, therefore, be transformed.

I'd like to explore what could be used to counter or challenge the symbolic constructions that support the state's repressive apparatus. As I stated previously, I am in no way seeking to defend a position that attacks, in one way or another, the idea of law, the state, or even sanctions. But, at the same time, it would be unreasonable to *preemptively* limit the shape and direction of a critical study. I'd like to try to determine what other representations of crime, punishment, and sanction can be devised and what other conceptions of the law advanced in order to, by comparison, understand the foundations of the modern judicial system.

Considering alternative ways to think about justice, and notably what a more "just" form of it might look like, isn't a localized question. It provokes broader questions and prompts us to reimagine the concept of crime, obviously, but especially, and more generally, concepts of nation, society, totality, political community, state, and law. Ultimately, challenging the system of penality requires the invention of a new language to understand the ways in which we engage with the world and our actions, a language different from that of Rousseau, Kant, and, later, Durkheim. We need to question the way in which those authors, and the state itself, employ categories of the social sciences or political philosophy.

DISMANTLING PENALITY

Instruments for devising a counterattack against the idea of a penal state and the apparatus of punishment can be found in the neoliberal tradition. This statement may, of course, be surprising and even shocking at first. And granted, neoliberalism is, in a sense, an individualist tradition, which adheres to the idea of the responsible individual that I mentioned in the previous section. For that reason it supports one of the two components of our judicial system—the system of judgment.

If, however, we apply neoliberal analysis to the second component, the system of punishment, it produces critical results. Its rejection of substantialist and abstract categories allows for a conception of action that is positioned in diametrical opposition to that on which the penal apparatus is based. From this perspective the neoliberal approach mirrors critical sociology in its project to challenge the structures of power.

If we read, for example, economist Gary Becker's seminal texts on crime and punishment,[1] it's clear that their underlying objective is to reject the relevance of transcendent totalities ("public order,"

---

1. Gary Becker, *The Economic Approach of Human Behaviour* (Chicago: University of Chicago Press, 1976), 39–85.

"state," "society") that undergird the repressive use of the law and to restore actions and their consequences to what they really are, meaning singular events or facts: a criminal act is an interpersonal interaction in which one individual wrongs another. A crime is a lateral and local matter that brings together victims and guilty parties, not, as modern law would have us believe, individuals and the state, individuals and society, or individuals and the law.

Becker proposes a new—economic—definition of crime that opposes the penal definition. I'm tempted to say that he formulates a reality that breaks with the falsifying representation of crime operated by the repressive state apparatus: a crime is not a public matter that offends, say, "society" or the law. It's a private matter. Ultimately, claims Becker, we could say that victims are nothing more than involuntary creditors. This viewpoint leads to the logical conclusion that the sole objective of the "sanction" determined by the law must be to reimburse that "credit," meaning to offer reparation for the harm or injury caused. The juridical reaction to crime should take the form of an obligation to repair the objective and subjective harm done to the victim. Damages therefore become the favored "punishment."

This conception leads to a strong critique of punitive practices, of the repressive conception of the law, and therefore, most notably, of the supplementary and expiatory punishment that is prison (or, in certain cases, fines). In a text published in 2011, Becker, responding to the question of whether there are too many people in prison, answered "yes." His full response was, of course, measured and cautious—and he was right. For Becker, prison appears necessary for certain crimes or criminals. Nonetheless, there are too many imprisoned individuals. That excess can be explained by two primary reasons: first, too many acts are defined as crimes when they shouldn't be, and therefore shouldn't lead to punishment by the state (Becker is thinking about "victimless crimes," and in particular, the issue of drugs); and second, prison is used excessively as an instrument to sanction. For crimes or infractions that cause limited harm and are easily repaired, damages are a much more appropriate punishment—and much less costly to society.[2]

Becker's ability to approach the question of crimes and sanctions in terms of their definition and implications in an innovative and, I must say, calm way comes from his adherence to the neoliberal tradition, which focuses primarily on the rejection of totalizing and transcendent approaches and of principles of sovereignty.[3] Neoliberal rationality is based on a refusal to accept the validity of a plane of reality higher than the discordant multiplicity of individuals and the relations between them. From this perspective there are only individuals and individual relationships.

Of course, the neoliberal viewpoint doesn't lead to the rejection of concepts like the state, the law, sanctions, bans, or courts. It in no way rejects those categories as if in a neoliberal society there were no more crime, aggression, law, punishment, or courts. Contrary to many anarchist utopias, the neoliberal utopia doesn't imagine the building of a future harmonious society but considers that society will always be characterized by opposition, conflict, harm to others, and the like.

But this system does provide new definitions of delinquency and of justice that contradict the state's construction of those concepts, which is visibly at work in the modern legal system. Neoliberal rationality, and all the more so libertarianism, is individualizing. It perceives rape, theft, injury, and attack *for what*

---

2. Gary Becker, "Does America Imprison Too Many People? Becker," *The Becker-Posner Blog*, Dec. 4, 2011, www.becker-posner-blog.com/2011/12/does-america-imprison-too-many-people-becker.html.

3. See Geoffroy de Lagasnerie, *La Dernière leçon de Michel Foucault: Sur le néolibéralisme, la théorie et la politique* (Paris: Fayard, 2012).

they are: private, singular matters that, each time they occur, are invariably lived in a specific manner by the agents involved. The function of the law should therefore be to institute sanctions and compensation *for the injury inflicted.* The notion of horizontal, compensatory, or reconstructive law replaces criminal and vertical law. We have here a complete rejection of the idea, so essential to the state apparatus, that rape, theft, injury, and aggression constitute, above all else, disruptions of the public order, that they are acts contrary to society's interests and should be punished for that very reason. The vision of crime as an act that disrupts society and the resulting belief in the legitimacy of criminal proceedings that can be launched by the public prosecutor's office in parallel with civil proceedings undertaken by the victim, or against the victim's wishes, or even when there is no victim (the example of drug-related offenses is most often cited in this respect), appear as artificial constructions through which the state consolidates a certain political order and affirms its self-proclaimed right to exercise control over our lives.

SOCIAL STATE, PENAL STATE, NEOLIBERAL STATE

Highlighting the cohesion between neoliberal rationality and a critique of the penal apparatus leads to a rather radical questioning of an analysis that has dramatically permeated the study of transformations of the power economy of contemporary societies.

One of the most firmly established arguments to date effectively maintains that, since the end of the 1970s, we have been witnessing a transformation of the state's role. Slowly but surely, measure by measure, we are said to be witnessing an intensification of states' repressive actions, in both Europe and the United States, through the transition from "social state" to "penal state." That change is presented as a consequence of the dismantling of a social vision of the world in favor of an individualizing one: the neoliberal vision. From this perspective neoliberalism constitutes a developing utopia whose principal tenets invalidate what Pierre Bourdieu calls the "left hand" of the state: social justice, redistribution, interventionism, collective solidarity, public assistance, and so forth. It is built on a logic of the individual, that is, on individual responsibility and "merit." It undoes bonds of solidarity and feelings of shared belonging that make it possible to intervene in the name of social justice. Neoliberalism favors the dismantling of insurance and redistribution on the basis of an economic or moral critique (by Friedrich Hayek or Robert Nozick, for example) of taxation and assistance in the name of the supposed superiority of a society in which everyone can do what they want with their bodies and jobs and in which the state does not have the right to dispossess individuals of what they have freely acquired.

This individualist logic within the economic sphere is said to lead to a deterioration of the social state. This is a well-known argument (formulated in 1939 by Georg Rusche and Otto Kirchheimer in their classic work on punishment): the rise in poverty provoked by the dismantling of social mechanisms produces anomic phenomena—increases in minor or major infractions, disorders, varied kinds of trafficking—and therefore a rise in delinquency and punishment.[4]

But, the argument continues, the impact of neoliberalism is not limited to a quantitative increase in illegal activity. It contributes above all to legitimizing the notion of sanctions and supporting an intensified punishment of infractions and crimes: this outlook,

---

4. See Georg Rusche and Otto Kirchheimer, *Peine et structure sociale* (Paris: Cerf, 1994), 113. [The most recent edition of the seminal *Punishment and Social Structure*, first published by Columbia University Press in 1939, is the Routledge edition of 2003.—Trans.]

based on individual responsibility, leads to the belief that there is no "excuse" for delinquency and that punishment is normal. The way to fight illegal activity is to force individuals to choose the "right track" by augmenting the cost of committing a crime: increasing sentences, refusing clemency, delivering more punishments. The idea is that a punitive apparatus dissuades criminals. Hence the insistence on the need to ensure a strong penal state to ensure the social order.

According to this analytical framework, neoliberalism has contributed less to a weakening of the state than to a transformation of its functions: from social state to penal state, left hand of the state to right, social treatment of poverty to penalization of poverty (punishment of the poor).[5]

Bernard Harcourt recently suggested a somewhat different way of understanding the existence of a link between neoliberal logic and the practice of penality and mass incarceration. He maintains that the idea that the economy should be organized by a free and decentralized market without government interference is necessarily coupled—and historically has always been coupled—with a discourse that valorizes and demands state intervention to reprimand individuals whose actions threaten the market order. The delinquent or criminal is perceived as an individual who endangers the normative foundations of a market society (property, respect for others' wants, nonviolence): his actions disrupt or interfere with competition between agents; they threaten the smooth functioning of liberalism. Neutralizing this individual is therefore necessary to ensure the liberal order. The concepts of laissez-faire and penality, a neoliberal state and a penal state, are therefore intrinsically linked:

---

5. See Pierre Bourdieu, "La démission de l'État," in *La Misère du monde* (Paris: Seuil, 1993), 337–50. See also "De l'État social à l'État pénal," special issue of *Actes de la recherche en sciences sociales* 124 (Sept. 1998).

they represent two sides of the same governmentality that valorizes the free market system. That is why Harcourt talks about a "neoliberal penality."[6]

The vision of history that contrasts the social state with the penal state and links penality and neoliberalism is convincing. It ties a system of conceptual oppositions to a historical narrative and clearly grasps the way in which state actions can deploy contradictory theoretical constructions. This vision describes a conflict between individualization and socialization, between the logic of responsibility and the logic of solidarity. From this perspective liberal policy causes economic precarity and the rise of inequality whereas social policy favors assistance and social justice. The result is a choice between a strong penal state, on one hand, and a social state, on the other.

In the previous section I myself produced an analysis that shows how the theoretical frameworks of the social state can be defined as antagonistic to those that undergird the penal state, such that I, too, played on an opposition between social state and penal state. And I maintain that if we consider how they conceive of action and of what takes place "out there," we are indeed dealing with two antagonistic apparatuses that shape different perspectives on the world, have distinct ways of handling and reacting to events, and from there, either make possible the system of judgment or, on the contrary, oblige us to question it.

But things are never so simple, and this opposition can be nuanced. From another point of view, the opposition social state/penal state can be questioned and criticized as neither subtle nor specific enough. Even if it is relevant to an understanding of the system of judgment, the contradictions and different principles at work within

---

6. Bernard Harcourt, *The Illusion of Free Markets: Punishment and the Myth of Natural Order* (Cambridge, MA: Harvard University Press, 2011).

the state mean that this opposition cannot provide critical tools sufficient to fully grasp the other dimension of our justice system, the practice of punishment.

Contrasting the social state and the penal state by associating the latter with individualism, neoliberalism, the destruction of solidarity, and the like means completely bypassing the basis and justification for penal repression: the "Hegelian-Durkheimian" vision of society or the "Rousseauist-Kantian" vision of the state as transcendent authorities. *Punitive practices presuppose the idea of "society." Without those socializing abstractions there is no penality.* If modern transformations of the state had truly been driven by a neoliberal logic, they wouldn't have taken the form of a strengthening of the penal state. Individualizing, neoliberal logic functions as a critique of penality and its underlying concepts (as we see in the work of Becker), whereas a certain application of a collective vision supports the apparatus of punishment. We're therefore dealing with correlations that run contrary to those that are traditionally assumed. The penal state *is* a social state. It invokes social categories. Consequently, we cannot strictly oppose the penal state and the social state or link the penal state and neoliberalism. For neoliberalism doesn't favor the principles of the penal state but rather, in part, its dismantling.

Pierre Bourdieu wasn't wrong when he said that the neoliberal program entails the destruction of collectives.[7] This agenda of dismantling transcendent authorities, viewed as theoretical fictions and political dangers, entails a dismantling of the social state—though not of every possible form of redistribution. But that individualizing vision also entails reassessing the penal state and the logic of punishment. In other words, if neoliberalism does indeed constitute a program that destroys collectives, we should add that,

---

7. See Pierre Bourdieu, "L'essence du néolibéralisme," *Le Monde diplomatique*, March 1998, repr. in *Contre-Feux* (Paris: Raisons d'agir, 1998), 108–19.

conversely, social vision constitutes a program that constructs collectives. And these actions can, depending on the case, have positive or negative effects.

As a result, the political question cannot be reduced to that of the collective versus individual, "sociology" versus "neoliberalism," the social vision versus the neoliberal-penal vision. Instead, we must question the meaning, effects, and consequences of the construction or destruction of this or that collective. Why build it, and why build it in this or that way? How? What effects does it produce? In short, the meaning of a given collective must be evaluated. Some uses of the notion of "collective" liberate, ensure, protect. But others alienate, constrain, disable, suppress. Most do all that simultaneously. There's not much point in being "for" or "against" the destruction or construction of collectives. In every case, we need to question the effects of inclusion and of the creation of apparatuses of socialization and belonging.

Any emancipatory intellectual endeavor must operate strategically. It can therefore be driven, according to circumstances and situations, to use instruments that may, at first glance, appear contradictory. Because the penal state individualizes causes in order to judge, critiquing the workings of the law requires us to reflect on the violent effects produced by that concealment of social forces. But because the state socializes interindividual actions and their effects in order to punish, we must contrast it with a vision that dismantles the perceptions established by totalizing concepts such as society, collective consciousness, and the like. So, on the one hand, we are dealing with an opposition between a sociological vision and an individualizing one and, on the other, with a left-libertarian vision and a socializing one.*

---

* See the footnote following the opening paragraph of Chapter 3.—Trans.

We can appreciate this uncomfortable situation by invoking the fact that the world (and, in this case, the state) isn't coherent or ordered, that it can obey contradictory logics, which means, by extension, that our emancipatory endeavor must also be deployed using approaches that may appear contradictory but that, in fact, share a strategic objective: to evaluate power structures and diminish the general quantity of violence.

That said, I should also emphasize that here we are in fact dealing with the two major visions that arise from a sociological approach—visions that can at times appear contradictory and that explain the tensions present in the political practices that claim to reflect social analyses. Sociology demonstrates, on the one hand, the intensity of social determinations and the prescriptive force of mechanisms of socialization. From this perspective all individualizing discourse is violent because it prevents us from considering events and our actions as the actualization of structural and global processes (critiques of the system of judgment fall under this kind of reflection). But on the other hand, sociology also reveals the constraints placed on us by social groups and imposed affiliations or belonging and the struggles present within the range of relationships we establish (familial, friendly, economic, etc.). From this perspective socializing discourse is violent because it prevents us from seizing the means with which to liberate ourselves from the collectives to which we belong or to undo the power effects that arise from our submission to transcendent logics (the critique of the system of punishment reflects this vein of thought).

PENALITY AND SOVEREIGNTY

The idea of law endorsed by the left-libertarian vision—a law that is quite simply not penal, a law limited to overseeing mechanisms of restitution and interindividual compensation—is difficult, perhaps impossible, to imagine and appears to lack all practical sense when it comes to those offenses that involve aggression and injury to others: rape, assault and battery, and in particular manslaughter and murder. With what compensation could such injuries be "repaired"? In other words, I am in no way saying that the only legitimate form of justice is restorative or civil rather than criminal—particularly because one of our objectives is precisely to imagine a type of justice that would avoid these well-known forms and would position itself outside the logic of compensation and punishment.

Instead, I'd like to demonstrate that it is possible to use this hypothetical, and perhaps even this aspiration for lateral justice, in which the state would only intervene as an arbiter to evaluate and rule on private conflicts, rather than as an accusing party, to identify the principles that support the construction of the penal apparatus. The notion of a civil, horizontal, and singular form of law provides instruments for revealing what, conversely, underpins and is at stake within the logic of repression: How to explain that construction? On behalf of what power system does it operate? I'd also like to show how the question of penality opens the way to a broader reflection on the contemporary political order and the state—in other words, how it is our political condition as a subject of law and of the state that is at stake in the system of judgment.

The left-libertarian view of the law lets us see that the penal state is a technique intended to fetishize the law and to instill in us subjects a disposition for obedience and submission. Granted, crime is defined as an act of transgression in both the left-libertarian and penal conceptions of the law. But the definition of the law and, therefore, that of its transgression are not identical; they are, in fact, contradictory. In the liberal conception the law isn't an autonomous system, valuable in and of itself; rather, it is a juridical transcription of the protection of the ownership rights that apply to our person and belongings. Violating the law, then, isn't problematic as such. Indeed, from this perspective there's nothing serious about violating the law. What's problematic is that this transgression consists of causing loss or injury to someone else.

The penal conception held by the criminal justice system, however, reflects an authoritarian ethic: it valorizes a pure ethic of conformity, an attitude of obedience for obedience's sake. It presents crime as a challenge to the law that must be punished *for that very transgression*. The violation of the law is the problem in itself. The criminal justice apparatus thus considers a conviction to be a restoration of the authority of the law over individuals designated as rebellious or disobedient. Criminal justice practices reject an awareness of acts as they objectively and truly are in order to establish, when it comes to punishment, a warlike scene pitting the state and its authority on one side against individuals and their dissident tendencies on the other. This cannot but lead to excessive and irrational consequences such as, for example, the sentencing of an individual, in the name of the public order, to twenty years in prison for stealing forty-five thousand euros during a robbery on the grounds that, as a repeat offender, he demonstrates a disregard for the law that requires exemplary punishment and a call to order.[8]

The core element of a left-libertarian—and, I believe, democratic—conception is the affirmation that it is uniquely because there is a victim that there is a crime, because the existence of a victim attests to the existence of a crime, meaning that the true nature of the damage or harm caused, and it alone, should determine the nature and extent of the sanction. The law and the judiciary intervene only secondarily, as apparatuses dedicated to the organization

---

8. See "Pour des vols de survie, Philippe Lalouel risque la prison à perpétuité," *Politis*, Jan. 28, 2014, www.politis.fr/articles/2014/01/pour-des-vols-de-survie-philippe-lalouel-risque-la-prison-a-perpetuite-25460/.

of sanctions and the reparation of damages: they are instruments at the service of individuals and their rights. But the penal vision positions the law as the foremost authority. Crime exists because the law exists; furthermore, victims exist because the law exists, because the state plays the role of victim in any violation of the law. In short, the law doesn't matter here because it protects individuals but because it springs from the state.

This representation of the law serves to establish the state and juridico-political order as looming authorities of singular importance. For that reason, I believe that we can't understand the meaning of criminal justice unless we reembed it in a more general economy of powers. To think about penality, we can't limit ourselves to a juridical point of view or focus on the issue of crime and illegal activity. We need to think in terms of political rationality.

When Foucault analyzes the traditional structure of the construction and affirmation of the king's power in *Discipline and Punish*, he emphasizes that this system reveals itself the most clearly in the dialectics of crime and punishment. The logic of sovereignty is connected to the representation of a power that claims to be transcendent and superior and that aims to impose itself as such on its subjects. Sovereignty was therefore tied to the construction of a new definition of delinquency. All illegal activity appeared to be acts that challenged the king's authority—and the king himself. A king could therefore not remain indifferent to transgressions, which had to provoke a violent reaction on his part. Penality took on a juridico-political function: "It is a ceremonial by which a momentarily injured sovereignty is reconstituted." Before being a legal act, the "public execution" was a political act that "restore[d]" sovereignty "at its most spectacular."[9]

---

9. Michel Foucault, *Discipline and Punish*, trans. Alan Sheridan (New York: Vintage, 1995), 48.

We know that many of the analyses in *Discipline and Punish* maintain that modernity consisted of the disappearance of sovereignty to the advantage of a new power structure, which was lateral and dispersed, horizontal and silent—namely, discipline.

But did we really leave the era of sovereignty behind? Isn't the power exerted over us still a sovereign power, or doesn't it struggle to remain so? Shouldn't we, based on Foucault, yet despite him, reaffirm a theory of the state as the center and locus of power?

Penality confronts individuals with a transcendent authority (society, the state) and is built on a rationality completely outside the register of private interactions. During a trial the presence of the prosecutor, who poses as the victim and speaks on behalf of "society," symbolizes the fact that the world of penality is autonomous from the world of interactions and is based on a rupture with individual wills: there can be penal action without civil action, or a crime without a victim, and, in the same way, forgiveness is impossible; consent doesn't nullify the infraction. The law constructs itself by claiming to possess its own rationality. It functions as a transcendent system that imposes itself on us from the outside. The criminal justice machine and the state's repressive apparatus as we know them are not obvious or natural frameworks: they represent the modes through which a specific and historically situated power—sovereign power—is exercised. Through those modes the state produces effects of subjection, domination, and imposition.

Sociologist Nils Christie is right to say that, through the logic of the criminal justice system, the state steals from us. Or, more precisely, it steals conflicts from individuals: each time a private conflict emerges, or an aggression takes place, the state makes it its own. It dispossesses the concerned parties of the conflict in which they were involved. It expels the victim and establishes itself in his or her place; it imposes its legal categories, modes of perception, and designations; and it determines a mode of settlement that the two parties are forced to accept, and to which they must submit, regardless of their preference or desire. This mode of settlement (procedure, sentencing, and so on) can be unsatisfying to both parties. It renders impossible the application of any other logics, such as those of forgiveness, reparation, and agreement, which would allow the actors the possibility to negotiate a resolution to their conflict themselves—and perhaps, above all, to *define for themselves what "a resolution to their conflict" would mean*. Criminal justice signifies that the state appropriates private conflicts and dispossesses actors of the ability to negotiate and determine "sanctions" according to their own terms, desires, and "needs." Christie thus describes lawyers and judges as "professional thieves" and judicial categories as instruments with which the state dispossesses us of our own experiences.[10]

DEMOCRACY

Clearly then, we can ask ourselves to what extent penality conflicts with the requirements of democracy and the juridical transformations they impose. The idea of democracy is linked to what we can call an immanent conception of the state and the law that rests on the desire to establish a government for the people by the people. But self-governance through the state entails dissolving transcendent entities—bringing down sovereign power and deconstructing the idea that it could have its own interests in relation to "us."[11] In a democracy our relationship to politics and law cannot be one of dispossession. This requires a refusal of all apparatuses that might

---

10. See Nils Christie, "Conflicts as Property," *British Journal of Criminology* 17, no. 1 (1977): 1–15.
11. For more on the relationship between democracy, criticism, and immanence see Didier Eribon, *D'une révolution conservatrice et de ses effets sur la gauche française* (Paris: Léo Scheer, 2007); and "Réponses et principes," in "Autour de Didier Eribon: Class and Sexuality," special issue of *French Cultural Studies* 23, no. 2 (2012): 151–64.

lead to the state's obedience to logics beyond the awareness or understanding of its subjects. Democratic logic calls for the edification of a utilitarian conception of the state and an instrumental conception of the law. The state must be a tool in the service of individuals, its unique goal to guarantee and protect their rights.

But the state hasn't renounced sovereignty. It continues to deploy strategies to maintain its sovereign authority and perpetuate the image of and relationship to the law on which that rationality is built. The existence of punitive law and practices can be seen as a strategy by the state, or state apparatus, to resist democratic requirements in order to maintain a predemocratic functioning of power. Once again, we understand why it is doubtful that the contemporary rise of penality and punishment is a consequence of neoliberal ideology. In many respects that rise should be analyzed as a way for states to regenerate mechanisms of sovereignty at a time when they should be challenged, and indeed are being challenged, by democratic requirements. The logic of penality and punishment emerges when the state, instead of accepting the limited role of mediator or instrument, wants to continue to exist as a separate entity that can legitimately decree and then defend the application of a law that can sometimes be applied despite, and even against, individuals themselves—which leads to the attribution of an expiatory, rather than solely compensatory, function to the justice system.

If being democratic means dissolving sovereignty and, more generally, dismantling, to the extent possible, the apparatuses that attempt to conduct our conduct, then we are necessarily obliged to go as far as possible in the dissolution of the criminal justice apparatus—and in the depenalization of the law and justice. That doesn't mean, as we've seen, the disappearance of law or justice. Rather, it is essential that we affirm the necessity and possibility of conceiving of a way to handle illegal activity that would free itself from the logic of penality.

I'm well aware that it's very difficult to imagine the possible forms of a system organized to respond to aggressions or injuries other than those instituted by the system of judgment and punishment: accusation by the prosecution, court appearance, the imposing of liability, punishment, and possibly confinement. Yet criminal law and criminal justice are not intangible systems; they are embedded in a specific moment and linked to a specific political rationality—meaning that if it's true that punitive technology is one manifestation and one aspect of the historical exercise of power that is sovereignty, then democracy, insofar as it redefines politics and the state, necessarily calls for the imagination of a new kind of law and a new kind of justice.

Clearly this doesn't mean moving backward, toward systems of private justice, but, on the contrary, using the state to invent more lateral and singular modes of handling responses to aggressions, which would take place in the context of reconstruction and grant actors the ability to attribute autonomous meanings to what happens to them and affirm the possibility of forgiveness, negotiation, compensation, and speaking on one's own behalf. This new system could, for both the victim and the guilty party, give rise to another relationship to the world, to oneself, to injuries than that imposed on us by the system of punishment, produce a form of justice that would no longer entirely obey classic logics of restitution and repression, and that could even—why not?—take different forms depending on circumstance and individual desires.

This democratic and pluralist conception of the law and justice could allow us to overcome the tension that Jacques Derrida highlights in *Force of Law*.[12] Derrida notes that there is always an excess of justice in relation to the law, a "tension" between the prin-

---

12. Jacques Derrida, "Force of Law," in *Acts of Religion*, ed. Gil Anidjar, trans. Mary Quaintance (New York: Routledge, 2002), 230–98.

ciples of the law and actions taken by justice: the law is deployed in an abstract, universal, and general manner, whereas justice always deals with singularities, concrete cases, and unique situations to be handled as such.

But, in fact, Derrida only views that tension as insurmountable because he treats the forms of law as we know them and as they are imposed on us as if they were the only forms of law. Unthinkingly, many of us do the same. What would it mean to invent another kind of law, one that wouldn't function according to abstractions and generalizations or standardize forms and vocabularies? Can we imagine a just law—an immediately pluralist and fragmentary type of law—that, rather than imposing a unique procedure, gives actors the chance to define for themselves what has happened, how they have experienced it, and what it means to administer justice? We must embark on a path to construct a fully democratic form of law—meaning, quite simply, a state and a juridical regime that no longer function as a sovereign power.

We have yet to see anything of the sort.

PART FIVE
SEE THE WORLD

RETHINK SOCIOLOGY

When I began to think about this work and to embark on a study of justice and the categorization of criminal offenses, my intention was "ethnographic," in the established meaning of the term. I wanted to narrate trials, describe how criminal proceedings unfold, and observe how individuals are judged and what that means in terms of lived experiences; I wanted to present the way in which interactions among defendants, lawyers, prosecutors, witnesses, judges, and jurors take place; I wanted to question these actors and restore their points of view. My project was therefore formed in accordance with the classical definition of empirical sociology: define an object, use qualitative or quantitative investigative methods (in this case observation and interviews), and then reassemble the results in the form of a scientific analysis of reality.

As is clear, I completely gave up on that initial project. I distanced myself from the established investigative modes of the social sciences. What I have taken away from this research, from a methodological and epistemological point of view, is the extent to which the critical approach is incompatible with what we mean, in the humanities and social sciences, when we talk about ethnography, fieldwork, or observation, and indeed a certain use of statistics. These methods, which present themselves as ways to approach reality, in fact constitute obstacles to doing so: they prevent us not only from explaining or understanding reality but even, quite simply, from *seeing* it. Any approach that wants to comprehend the world as it is and deconstruct its mechanisms must break with the definition that an extensive tradition within the social sciences assigns itself.

I decided to dedicate a part of this book to a reflection on the conditions for the creation of a lucid (meaning critical and non-mystifying) perception of reality. What does it mean to investigate, and what does it mean to see the world? How should we proceed in order to understand events and actions and avoid established mystifications and ideologies?

INVESTIGATION

The traditional practice of sociological research relies on a naive perception of what it means to describe the world. It constitutes, to a certain extent, a simple extension of common sense and echoes the spontaneous manner in which any individual who wants to understand the world proceeds: seek out, investigate, transcribe. Researchers assign themselves the task of investigating parcels or fragments of reality whose description and study they purport to be undertaking. Their research subjects are real objects, preconstructed and open to investigation: this or that social or historical phenomenon, this or that type of actor or category, this or that institution or activity—an approach I suggest we call object-based thinking.

Granted, an adherence to naive empiricism or the belief in the possibility of "pure" observation stripped of all "preconstruction" is fortunately no longer possible, and nobody dares defend that position anymore. But this doesn't mean that theory, or even speculation, has been granted a role in the development of an investigation. The preference is for "method" or, as it's called in the Anglo-American social sciences, a theoretical framework, which has produced an abundance of scholarship. Method confers a semblance of construction and coherence to an empirical investigation. It serves to frame and structure a study but never to question reality and what is real.

I believe we should be extremely suspicious of this kind of approach because there is a contradiction between the search for the truth and the notion of an investigation that presents itself as wanting to provide a description of one segment of society. In other words, we need to reevaluate the role of ethnography, fieldwork, and observation in the critical tradition.

Even though I concentrate on ethnography and observation here, my criticism applies equally to studies that use qualitative methods and to those that use quantitative methods. This is because what I mean to challenge is, more broadly speaking, a way of defining and practicing the social sciences as an endeavor that, to gain awareness of the world, needs to carve out specific realities and study partial objects of the social world. In other words, I don't contrast specific and general, or the field and theory: it goes without saying that there are local and global elements, fieldwork, method, and theory everywhere and in every kind of study. My aim in this final chapter is to contrast two forms of thought: object-based thinking versus system-based and problem-based thinking.

STRUCTURE

The ethnographic stance purports to incarnate a project of perception; it would like to "show" reality. It always legitimizes itself by invoking its mission and ambition to demonstrate that which is real. In the same way, it tries to pass itself off as critique: it supposedly reconstitutes social life, objectively, against spontaneous perceptions, ideologies, media creations, and so on. But in truth this approach represents a self-delusion and acts as a blinding and neutralizing principle that organizes the absence of elements necessary to an understanding and explanation of the social world. It is obfuscatory, uncritical, and unable to produce any real and intelligible vision of the forces operating in social life. It observes but sees nothing. Object-based thinking leads to the proliferation of redundant or tautological analyses of the world.

The need to resist the ethnographic temptation and question the validity of any partial study stems, first, from the need to approach the social world in terms of systems and totalities. The validity of the reality reconstituted by any descriptive partial study can be challenged because the "facts" can never have meaning as such. They don't exist prior to their construction according to and based on a general theory, since that very theory enables their existence and determines what will count as facts. Adorno writes that "the facts are neither final nor impenetrable, even though the prevailing sociology regards them as such in accordance with the model of sense data found in earlier epistemology. In them there appears that which they are not."[1] What appears and what is at work in the background is society as a whole (constituted by class, exploitation, market systems, etc.), which "necessarily *transcends* its scattered facts" and can only be identified by breaking with "empirical findings."[2] Phenomena can only be attributed meaning within a general framework. Yet that framework is precisely not something that can be observed but is what must construct, organize, and shape observation. It eludes empirical meaning and must be elaborated and, we might say, theoretically affirmed. Observation protocols should be established according to that framework. Otherwise,

---

1. Theodor W. Adorno, "Introduction," *The Positivist Dispute in German Sociology*, trans. Glyn Adey and David Frisby (New York: Harper and Row, 1976), 11.
2. Theodor W. Adorno, "Sociology and Empirical Research," in ibid., 68 (emphasis added).

the sociologist is destined to understand neither the meaning of the facts he or she observes nor their organization and logic.

The idea that sociological thought can only be structural and totalizing, and that it therefore cannot accept the validity of individualizing studies that necessarily sideline their purported object, appears in Pierre Bourdieu's *Distinction*. Bourdieu shows the extent to which the meaning of the most quotidian and trivial actions, and the most particular preferences, cannot be understood unless they are reembedded in a general context of preferences and actions, which itself must be contextualized in relation to social classes, the general logics of domination, the functioning of the educational system, the distribution and transmission of capital (economic, cultural, social), relationship to time, and so forth.

Consequently, the cultural practices specific to each group, and that localized studies may have wanted to study individually, acquire meaning and make sense only when they are embedded in the system from which they emerged and that operates in a concealed manner. Henceforth, it is that system that should be reconstructed, using a theoretical approach, if we want to understand what's at stake in what we call reality. Background and structures are more *real* than daily and local interactions. The former determine and support the latter, and they are what must be reconstituted. So-called fieldwork, be it qualitative or quantitative—and what I call object-based thinking—cannot, by definition, grasp the global stage on which interactions take place or the structure in which each particular setting is embedded and from which it draws its objective meaning. This approach can therefore only produce superficial studies that overlook the essential and deflect attention from the only pertinent elements.

In my case, it was in a somewhat different way that I came to the belief that conducting a critical investigation means breaking with "descriptions" and "field research" as defined by sociology. Basically, I felt that taking as a point of departure that which offers itself as "real" to describe what is real prevents us from reconstituting the principles behind the construction of reality and the logics from which established forms derive and, therefore, from understanding what is truly at work in what presents itself as "real." This concern is particularly important when the object of study is institutions.

QUESTION WHAT'S REAL

The criminal justice system as we know it is the result of a specific way of responding to the problem of justice and of defining notions of crime, responsibility, judgment, victims, the law, and even plaintiffs. The act of judgment as it occurs in courtrooms every day deploys concepts of responsibility, penalty, neutrality, crime, justice, "victims," and finally punishment. Yet *these very concepts are not at stake during a trial*. A trial can only take place because those questions have been resolved and because the concepts have already been given specific meanings. The way in which they have been defined gives a trial its empirical form as it is experienced in the immediate. The trial form is the materialization of the way in which a society has responded to the problems inherent to the ideas of justice and penality and deduced a specific procedure. But those problems, by definition, no longer arise once the trial begins. The basic vision of the world that informs the institution of justice, and that makes the trial what it is, is never again raised, made explicit, or conceptualized as such. The actors all perform their roles within a fixed legal, political, and juridical framework. They debate by wielding and relying on shared categories. Each time a trial is held, there is an assumed consensus among parties about the state and judicial construction of the judicial sphere and the concepts on which it is based.

Grasping the reality of that system cannot consist of "going to see" and sharing what one perceives. This is because observation and ethnographic study, by their nature, are obligatorily incorporated *into a framework of interactions as it was institutionally imposed at a given time*. "Observational procedures" are confronted by a reality whose empirical actualization is drawn from principles of construction that are, by definition, no longer visible or presented as such. The empirical approach, therefore, can neither problematize nor question the bases of the observed scene. And no method, however rigorous, can correct this fundamental and original flaw. In a sense, everything unfolds as if embarking on "fieldwork" were the equivalent of accepting insertion within a space conceded and predetermined by the state (for example, the court such as it is, such as it is formed) and denying oneself the means with which to lead an investigation therein—that is, the means to disrupt the state's construction of reality (notions of penality, responsibility, repression, judgment).

I'd like to use an example to show the impasses inherent in any "ethnographic" approach and the way in which such an approach ensures an output of research that reinforces the state's construction of reality and established ideologies—namely, Didier Fassin's recent work, which interests me as both symptomatic and illustrative of a broader problem I will highlight. In preparation for this book I was naturally led to read Fassin's most recent publications, notably *Prison Worlds: An Ethnography of the Carceral Condition* and *Enforcing Order: An Ethnography of Urban Policing*, which focuses on anticrime units.[3] That I did so reveals just how difficult it is to construct an independent reflection that escapes prevailing cultural and academic opinion, the dictates they impose, and their blinding

---

3. Didier Fassin, *Enforcing Order: An Ethnography of Urban Policing* (Cambridge, MA: Polity, 2013); and Didier Fassin, *Prison Worlds: An Ethnography of the Carceral Condition* (Cambridge, MA: Polity, 2017).

effect, because, conversely, many books or articles essential to my thought process only struck me as such later on. I believed it obvious that I should read certain books and that they would help me in my project. But that was a mistake. I found reading this kind of research a disappointment whose cause it is important to understand in order to determine what writing criticism in the social sciences really means.

Fassin practices an observation-based sociology: he sets himself up in a prison or police station intending to produce its ethnography. In this way he says that he wants to increase public awareness of reality. He also presents his approach as driven by a "critical" ambition, which is in fact trivially reduced to exposing "truths" and therefore enabling a project of public deliberation and institutional reform. This is why, according to him, there is a link between ethnography and democracy.

Yet what struck me about his work was the extent to which his practice of "embedded sociology"—which isn't specific to him but represents one of the conventional kinds of fieldwork—dooms him to *being caught up in the ideology of the very institutions he believes to be his objects of study*. He accepts the official definition of those institutions, as well as their self-construction and self-attributed values. The police exist to ensure public order; prison is for punishment, self-improvement, and rehabilitation. Fassin builds his investigations on those ideologies. His studies boil down to a project to highlight how real practices represent "dysfunctions" of official missions, why institutions fail to accomplish their goals, and the way in which actors themselves create systems of justification to understand why their concrete actions don't correspond to what they are supposed to do (this is the sociology of "moral economies"). The normative horizon of ethnography is thus reduced to social and political orthopedics: make institutions do what they're supposed to do.

Fassin's book on prisons aims to show how discriminatory judging and incarceration practices reveal that "repression is not aimed toward equitable punishment" and therefore tends to "empty" the punishment, perceived as arbitrary and unjust, of its "meaning."[4] Repression in itself is never questioned or taken as the object of study. It is viewed as positive and necessary; its sole limitation is its unequal application. Fassin also maintains that carceral conditions (overpopulation, guard/prisoner interactions, idleness) prevent contemporary prisons from playing their "role"—whose official representation he therefore completely endorses—of rehabilitation and reform. For instance, with regard to the boredom that reigns in prison and the "structural shortage of activity" that leaves most inmates with nothing to do, the sociologist writes: "The sense of the pointlessness of the sentence time thus undermines the prison's designated mission, whether from the point of view of moral education or of social reintegration."[5] How can categories as naive as "moral education" or "social reintegration" be used in a book presented as a scholarly work? I've always been struck by the number of ideological notions and clusters at work in studies that nonetheless present themselves as "rational" and "empirical" and that thereby see themselves as falling into the category—spuriously contrasted with critique—of observation and science.

We find the same pattern in Fassin's book on anticrime squads. Observation is intended to reveal how the police apply unequal practices (according to skin color or social background) that go against the republican imperative of equality: the police should safeguard the public order. The problem is simply that, in practice, they strengthen the hierarchical social order. The following excerpt reveals the logic at work in what is nonetheless presented as a "so-

---

4. Fassin, *Prison Worlds*, 293.
5. Ibid., 128.

ciological analysis": "The fact that the law is not applied equally to all and that rights are not recognized as identical for everyone signifies a renunciation of the equality that is yet so emphatically trumpeted by institutions. The fact that, on the basis of their place of residence, the color of their skin, their assumed origin and their social background, individuals are presumed to be criminals . . . constitutes an assault on dignity that strikes at the heart of the very possibility of communities living together."[6]

One might think that the noncritical and conservative nature of Fassin's work has less to do with his method than with a world vision to which he adheres and which appears in his writing in notions inherited from social Christianity and bourgeois philanthropy such as "living together," "moral community," "moral rehabilitation," "social reintegration," and "dignity." But, more profoundly, I don't think it's possible to separate ethnographical approach from conservative vision because adopting a field-based approach implies accepting and maintaining the frameworks that organize social life. These two attitudes echo and complement one another. This prompts the question of whether a critical ethnography is possible and if the empirical, object-based definition of research can be compatible with a radical investigation of reality.

The ethnographic approach forces the researcher to situate himself *inside* and adhere to the institution in question and therefore to endorse its foundations. Ethnography is deployed (in the quasi-spatial sense) within the state's construction of reality. Defining one's project as ethnographic implies the researcher has renounced speculation and global thinking and therefore has prevented himself from asking critical questions about the foundations and meaning of the very institutions he believes to be his objects of study. A local-

---

6. Ibid., 222.

ized approach can only ask localized questions, meaning it embeds itself within and thereby ratifies forms of institutions, the essence of which will consequently never be questioned or challenged. Setting out to describe a partial object of the social and preconstructed world requires having renounced a deconstructive and problematizing approach that questions established frameworks of experience and politics (the same renunciation, tantamount to an act of self-mutilation, drives what is called the "sociology of justification").

Conversely, the critical approach always pursues a vastly different objective: to produce new visions of the world and new objects. In other words, ethnography implies that a noncritical desire is driving its author, who has accepted immersion in the world as it is and whose writing reflects an extension of existing and circulating ideologies.

It's hard not to be taken aback, in this respect, by the striking difference between Fassin's study on prisons and the questions raised by Foucault in *Discipline and Punish*. That gap reveals everything that separates a critical approach from a falsely, and ultimately mystifying, ethnographic one.

In *Discipline and Punish* Foucault does highlight the "dysfunctions" of prisons and the "failures" of confinement, notably the way in which the former contribute, despite their intentions, to recidivism or the construction of a delinquent milieu. But he doesn't simply treat those dysfunctions as failures or elements to be corrected through reform. He goes beyond the perceptions and designations that betray an adherence to established carceral ideologies and official visions and values. He asks further questions: Don't these constant, regular "dysfunctions" actually reveal the *truth* about prisons? Are the things we automatically perceive to be failures really failures? Or do they in fact represent *the purpose of prison* and what it seeks to generate? Are the production of recidivism and the creation of a delinquent milieu a dysfunction or, on the contrary, a *function* of the carceral universe?

Confronting these questions forces us to break from reality as it presents itself to experience, to take a step back. They lead us to problematize *the prison form itself* and to challenge the validity of carceral ideology and our beliefs in the functions of punishment and repression. Our object of study inevitably becomes that which underlies and defines the specific sociohistoric framework that is the carceral universe, which we then reembed in a broader economy of power in order to identify its true nature. When prison claims to reform a criminal (an official ideology that the sociology of moral economies erects as reference, truth, and point of departure), it in fact produces the delinquent individual as a specific identity.

This kind of thinking, as we've seen, is entirely absent from Fassin's books. Why? It is not by choice or omission but because the ethnographer is structurally incapable of exploring or even imagining those kinds of problems. Asking and answering such—critical—questions requires that we give ourselves the means to be in a position that *overlooks* the current construction of the carceral reality, whereas "field sociology," on the contrary, is situated beneath and within that framework. Fieldwork and empiricism are embedded in "what is," which amounts to an endorsement of the state's logic and complicity in its reproduction.[7] This is why I chose not to conduct any interviews while writing this book, be they with judges, lawyers, defendants, or jurors: the desire to understand the forces acting on us and the hope of identifying the unconscious structures of the system of judgment and punishment meant that such an approach would have, by definition, been pointless. From my perspective there is a contradiction between

---

7. See Pierre Bourdieu, *Raisons pratiques* (Paris: Seuil, 1994), 144.

sociological thinking and the idea of interviewing actors. Likewise, as the reader will have observed, there aren't many empirical examples in this work. My objective is not to describe but to think, meaning that when an example illustrates or proves a point, it's not necessary to cite another example on the same subject. We should use reality strategically rather than fetishize it as if it were an inherently valuable element.

The critique of empiricism I express here isn't uniquely applicable to sociology, ethnography, or anthropology. It has broad applications and targets a way of thinking and understanding reality that can be at work in every discipline. History is an obvious example. But I could just as easily have chosen economist Thomas Piketty's *Capital in the Twenty-First Century* to illustrate my point. That study's descriptive aim, in opposition to the modeling trend in economics, prompts Piketty to construct his project around a nontheorized and nonquestioned notion of capital. He reduces capital to what capitalism calls capital, that is, to what offers itself to our perception as such—namely, economic capital. This leads him to overlook and render invisible all other forms of capital present in society (cultural, educational, social, symbolic, etc.), to avoid other kinds of legacies as problematic, and therefore to produce a conservative vision of the social hierarchy that prevents an understanding of—when it does not mask and thereby endorse and legitimize—the real logic of domination and reproduction.[8] The way to escape that bias, which condemns Piketty's work to represent but a conceptual regression in a politically conservative vein, would be to construct a structural theory of the forms of capital—modeled on Pierre Bourdieu's *Distinction*. This would in turn have required

---

8. Thomas Piketty, *Le Capital au XXIe siècle* (Paris: Seuil, 2013). See my article "Le manifeste inégalitaire de Thomas Piketty," *Libération*, Oct. 17, 2013. Also see Alexis Spire, "Capital, reproduction sociale et fabrique des inégalités," *Annales* 70, no. 1 (2015): 61–68.

taking a theoretically informed and intellectually rigorous global and critical perspective of contemporary capitalism and liberal democracy and the corresponding ideologies that participate in their operation and perpetuation.

PROBLEMATIZE

My investigation of justice and the system of judgment should be taken as a proposal for a renewed method for philosophy and the social sciences, one that breaks with the tradition of "empirical" or field sociology as practiced in France or the United States, and even, more generally, with the idea of descriptive investigation as it may arise across all disciplines. We must substitute a problematic and problematizing approach for the methodological and "field"-based one, which in no way reproduces reality but rather ratifies established mystifications and past constructions.

Understanding criminal proceedings and revealing the logic systems at work during trials necessitates that we recreate penal categories and identify the "system of judgment" and the "system of repression," that is, the general apparatus of criminal law and the concepts it deploys and applies to us. Yet, because the system of judgment rests on a specific way of signifying a certain number of concepts—responsibility, penality, defense, repression, law, and the like—understanding what happens in that sphere requires that we problematize those ideas and ask ourselves what might be the different ways of considering them and how they, in fact, operate within our culture. That is what I have striven to do at every stage of this study. It is an approach that requires breaking with what presents itself as reality—what Bourdieu called "breaking with common sense"—in order to recover the true reality and reinscribe any observations in a field of questions and contingent problematics. These are some of the questions we should ask: What are the different possible ways of conceiving of responsibility? What are the different conceptions of crime? What other ways of judging or envisaging judgment and punishment can we imagine? If judging implies notions of "responsibility," "causality," "crime," "victimization," and "damages," then what meanings can we give those concepts; and what meanings do they, in fact, take on? According to what principles are we deemed judge-able and are we judged and punished? In short, what are the objective foundations of operations of judgment? What effects of power do those apparatuses exercise?

Ethnography is blind to these critical questions. It chooses not to see them or take them into consideration. That blindness is self-imposed: ethnography *situates itself in the space of answers* and rejects the questions as speculative, normative, or structural or determinist philosophy, whereas they should be the starting point for any investigation.

Sociology must be stripped of the temptation to define itself as an activity that studies objects. If we look at announcements for upcoming conferences or publications, it's striking that, in both Europe and the United States, papers and lectures are nearly always presented as contributions of documentary value. And we know that when sociologists, historians, or anthropologists meet, the first question they ask each other is "what is your field of study?" (and never, "what problem do you want to explore?" or "what is your perspective?"), which shows how research has been reduced to an activity characterized above all by the objects it studies. For that matter, professional associations and conferences are always organized by divisions into "thematic sections," as if "themes" constituted relevant criteria when considering research.

On the contrary, sociology should take the form of a reflection on stakes and questions. The social sciences must choose as subjects not *circumscribed realities* (even if they are examined using theories and methods) but *problems* to be confronted and illuminated with the help of analyses, readings, and examples that can come from different sectors. Being a sociologist does not mean setting out to study a given alimentary practice but rather thinking about "distinction" and the relative distribution of preferences and aversions. It's not about relating what occurs in this or that school, classroom, or group of students but reflecting on mechanisms of reproduction. It's not about describing a prison but questioning actions to "discipline and punish," not focusing on a given handicap but exploring stigmatization. (Erving Goffman's work *Stigma* is a particularly illustrative example of the kind of thought I believe essential, notably because it draws examples from such widely varied and heterogeneous domains across time and space—studies, novels, documents, etc.—to reflect on the problem his book takes up, namely, how identities viewed as "spoiled" are handled in the public space.) Similarly, my project isn't defined as the study of such-and-such a courtroom but as the investigation of the system of judgment and punishment.

IMAGINE

The need for the critical (and therefore more truthful) approach to take a problematizing and assertive form was recently justified by Joan W. Scott in "Gender: A Useful Category of Historical Analysis." Scott essentially asks on what conditions it is possible to construct a critical history of gender and gender relations. And she answers that question by maintaining that "gender," as it functions in our societies, cannot be understood as a "reality to be described," as if it sufficed to explore archives or make observations to realize how it functions. "Gender" or gender relations as they exist in a given place at a given time must, according to Scott, be considered as constituting a response given by a society to what she calls the "dilemma of sexual difference." I remain unconvinced by her wording, which ultimately presupposes as given the very thing she claims to want to problematize. But the method highlighted by Scott interests me and strikes me as important. Critically analyzing gender-based operations requires an approach that does not take the "real" as its point of departure. On the contrary, we have to *imagine what does not exist*. That means seeking out the multiple ways in which a society can handle the question of sexual difference and regulate the meaning of the body, individual relationships to desire, sexuality, the public space, and so forth. There are multiple ways of conceiving of "gender norms." And the "reality" of the gender-based operations at work in a society that we want to study becomes clearer through their historically observable divergence from those possibilities. What we call "gender" in one "society" must be conceptualized as one of many possible ways of treating the "dilemma of sexual difference." In other words, the critical approach requires that we begin with a problem (in this case "gender"), reflect on the possibilities it introduces and the real or hypothetical responses that may be found (Scott especially uses psychoanalysis as an instrument of imagination), before finally, in the end, describing the specific reality in which we live and its unconscious, contingent, and arbitrary foundations.[9] Critical work does, then, consist of descriptions, observations, "archives," and statistical data. But these aren't constituted as given in advance. Their relevance and significance are created by and arise from the theoretical endeavor and are in some way put at its service.

A problematizing endeavor allows us to present the world as we know it as one of many possible worlds, as one of many possible

---

9. Joan W. Scott, "Gender: A Useful Category of Historical Analysis," *American Historical Review* 91, no. 5 (1986): 1053–75.

ways to create the world. The scientific approach thus finds itself immediately charged with an ethical task. To produce knowledge, we must step back from ourselves because the more we want to know ourselves, the more we will be driven to change.